1,000,000 Books
are available to read at

Forgotten Books

www.ForgottenBooks.com

Read online
Download PDF
Purchase in print

ISBN 978-1-333-69589-7
PIBN 10536841

This book is a reproduction of an important historical work. Forgotten Books uses state-of-the-art technology to digitally reconstruct the work, preserving the original format whilst repairing imperfections present in the aged copy. In rare cases, an imperfection in the original, such as a blemish or missing page, may be replicated in our edition. We do, however, repair the vast majority of imperfections successfully; any imperfections that remain are intentionally left to preserve the state of such historical works.

Forgotten Books is a registered trademark of FB &c Ltd.
Copyright © 2018 FB &c Ltd.
FB &c Ltd, Dalton House, 60 Windsor Avenue, London, SW19 2RR.
Company number 08720141. Registered in England and Wales.

For support please visit www.forgottenbooks.com

1 MONTH OF FREE READING

at

www.ForgottenBooks.com

By purchasing this book you are eligible for one month membership to ForgottenBooks.com, giving you unlimited access to our entire collection of over 1,000,000 titles via our web site and mobile apps.

To claim your free month visit: www.forgottenbooks.com/free536841

* Offer is valid for 45 days from date of purchase. Terms and conditions apply.

English
Français
Deutsche
Italiano
Español
Português

www.forgottenbooks.com

Mythology Photography **Fiction** Fishing Christianity **Art** Cooking Essays Buddhism Freemasonry Medicine **Biology** Music **Ancient Egypt** Evolution Carpentry Physics Dance Geology **Mathematics** Fitness Shakespeare **Folklore** Yoga Marketing **Confidence** Immortality Biographies Poetry **Psychology** Witchcraft Electronics Chemistry History **Law** Accounting **Philosophy** Anthropology Alchemy Drama Quantum Mechanics Atheism Sexual Health **Ancient History Entrepreneurship** Languages Sport Paleontology Needlework Islam **Metaphysics** Investment Archaeology Parenting Statistics Criminology **Motivational**

Entered, according to Act of Congress, in the year 1920.
BY THE PUBLIC SCHOOL AUXILIARY,
In the Office of the Librarian of Congress, at Washington, D. C.

[ALL RIGHTS RESERVED]

COMMUNITY CHURCH AND FIRST SCHOOL
FREDERICKSBURG, TEXAS

THE FREDERICKSBURG

Home Kitchen Cook Book

Published by
THE PUBLIC SCHOOL AUXILIARY
OF FREDERICKSBURG, TEXAS

FIRST EDITION 1916
SECOND EDITION REVISED AND ENLARGED 1921

OFFICERS FOR 1920 to 1921

MRS. H. M. HARRINGTON, President
MRS. VICTOR KEIDEL, Vice-President
MRS. F. J. MAIER, Secretary
MISS ZULA MAE HILL, Treasurer

PREFACE.

The second edition of this book has been compiled in commemoration of the 75th anniversary of the founding of the town of Fredericksburg, and is lovingly dedicated by the

       Fredericksburg Public School Auxiliary,
              to those
          sturdy Pioneers,

whose indomitable spirit and energy have transformed a bit of Texas wilderness, into a place of peaceful abode and prosperity.

COOKING AND CULTURE ON THE PEDERNALES

The rolling prairie dripping with the violent torrential rains of Texas or seared and parched a dry and cracking brown by summers' drouth, the sparkling rivers with their sombre cypress borders or shady groves of walnut and pecan—know only woodland sounds of birds and beast that seek their cooling shelter, taste of the purling waters, browse on the succulent herbs and grasses or prey upon the weaker of their kind.

The nomad Indian prowls along these peaceful haunts, brings to earth the wild turkey with his bow and arrow, prepares the feast over the open fire and devours it resting on his haunches. After the meal he smokes his soothing "Calumet", its brown leaves, prairie-yielded. He teaches the stripling redskin how to fell the bison—to prepare the deadly arrow with the venom of the viper, — all his lore is slaying — slaying, for food, for shelter, for revenge, or conquest.

The first blow of the ax—tocsin of human progress. The pioneer has come to clear the land and build his rough log cabin. In the spacious fire-place swings the iron kettle with his rude trappers' fare; he rears a stalwart race, steeled to hard labor, untaught, unlettered save for the woodland crafts, the hunt, the stream or skirmishings with Indian neighbors.

In homespun cloth, astride on shaggy ponies, the lads and lasses wend their way to the log schoolhouse on the hillock, summoned by the peal of the forefather of all Texas school-bells. The master cloaks his lack of learning under greater sterness, the text-book playing second fiddle to the ferrule. Homes on the first thanksgiving can boast of bounteous cupboards; the hardest years are past and there is time for feast and song, for ease and plenty.

Thru snowy cotton fields, acres of corn and grain, traverse two tiny lines of steel on a ribbed bed of logs and the day at last has come that the last peg is to be put into the iron trail — a happy consummation!

The thriving town is decked with flags and bunting; schoolchildren, clad in Sunday laces, sing welcome to the throng that has come to christen the first engine destined to draw the products of their fields and orchards to the great marts of trade. Bands play and feasts are spread; the best of all that harvest yields is showered forth to tempt the appetite: huge cakes and fragrant pies and tarts, jellies and preserves all testify to housewives' skill; savory sausages, home cured hams and mellowest of cheese disclose their craft.

There is loud rejoicing here for what has been achieved and there is too, a still and holy joy for what is yet to be — and a few dreamers see, — nestled among these lovely hills — a city bright and fair, peaceful abode for a happy, healthy and industrious generation, led by wise council, and crowned by the fairest of all temples — a perfect SCHOOL-HOUSE.

RELISHES

Oyster Cocktail.

6 oysters; 2 tablespoonfuls tomato catsup; ½ teaspoonful of grated horse radish; juice of ½ small lemon; dash of Worcestershire Sauce.

This is for one cocktail.

MRS. F. L. FREY.

Pineapple Cocktail.

1 pineapple; ½ cupful orange juice; 1 cupful sugar; 1/3 cupful grapefruit juice; ½ cupful cocoanut; 1/3 cupful water.

Boil the sugar and water together for five minutes, cool, add the fruit juices. Cut fresh pineapple in cylinders, using an apple corer, put in glasses with cocoanut, and cover with the syrup.

MRS. ALFRED P. C. PETSCH.

Cheese Straws.

1 cup flour; 1 cup grated cheese; 1 level teaspoon salt; 1|6 teaspoon Cayenne pepper; 4 tablespoons melted Snowdrift (any kind of lard will do); 3 tablespoons ice water.

Sift flour and mix with Snowdrift stirring with a fork. Add cheese and seasoning, and lastly add ice water. Roll on floured board about ¼ inch thick. Cut into narrow strips and bake in quick oven.

MISS ALVINA GOLD.

Pimento and Egg Canapees.

Pimentos ½ can; butter ½ cup; salt ½ teaspoonful; eggs (hard boiled); bread; bread, toasted or fried; pickled walnuts, or any other pickles.

Rinse the pimentoes in cold water, dry on a cloth, then rub through a sieve, add the salt and butter and pound until whole is smooth. Spread on diamond-shaped pieces of toasted or fried bread, placing a slice of hard boiled egg and a small piece of pickle in the center of each piece of bread.

CONSTANCE STRIEGLER.

Stuffed Celery.

¼ lb. Roquefort cheese; ½ cup sweet cream; paprika, olives, green peppers.

Work cream into cheese until as smooth as paste; add chopped olives and peppers; fill hollows of tender stalks of celery, dust with paprika; serve as an appetizer with soup or as after-dinner cheese.

MRS. W. PETIT.

Anchovy Appetizer.

Spread triangles of toast with anchovy paste, place on each a thin slice of fresh ripe tomato, sprinkle over with hard boiled egg chopped fine. Place on nest of cress or parsley garnished with pimento strips.

MRS. H. GOLDSCHMIDT.

Table Mustard.

3 tablespoonfuls of mustard; 1 tablespoonful of butter; 1 tablespoonful of sugar; ½ cupful of vinegar; yolks of 2 eggs.

Wet mustard with a little boiling water, add sugar, yolks of eggs, well beaten, and vinegar. Mix well, set in boiling water for a few minutes, stirring. A good relish.

MRS. A. B. WILLIAMSON.

Welsch Rarebit.

1 tablespoonful of butter; 1 teaspoonful of cornstarch; ½ teaspoonful of mustard; salt and Chili pepper to taste; ½ cup of cream; ½ lb of soft mild American cheese.

Cream, butter, cornstarch and mustard to a paste. Add to the hot cream. Lastly add cheese and seasoning. Stir till cheese melts. Serve on toast browned on one side.

MISS DORA NAUWALD.

Ham Relish.

¼ lb cheese; ¼ lb boiled ham; 3 eggs; 6 ordinary square soda crackers.

½ pint milk; 1 teaspoon Worcestershire Sauce; ½ teaspoon baking powder. Use finest cutter of any meat chopper. Run cheese through first, then the ham and then the crackers. Add Worcestershire Sauce, red pepper and salt. Then add milk and mix thoroughly. Beat the eggs until very light, then add in the butter. Sprinkle baking powder over the top and mix it lightly. Bake showly in buttered earthen baking dish until brown.

MRS. A. ZINCKE.

Mexican Relish.

4 green tomatoes; 2 green peppers; 1 onion; ½ teaspoon horseradish, chop or grind fine. Place this in a jar and cover with boiling vinegar, to which 1 teaspoon salt, 2 tablespoon Chili Powder and 1 tablespoon mustard have been added. The Chili Powder should be boiled in the vinegar for at least ten minutes before the other seasoning is added.

To be served with any meat dishes.

MRS. HARRY HEYLAND.

Cheese Souffle.

2 eggs; 1 cup of grated cheese; 1 cup of sweet milk; 1 heaping tablespoonful of flour; pinch of salt.

Put in buttered pan, cook in hot oven ten minutes.

MRS. HARRY M. HARRINGTON.

SOUPS

Beef Soup.

Boil 2 ℔ of beef in ½ gal. water. When it has come to a boil, skim and add salt and pepper to taste, a pinch of celery salt, 1 onion, and 1 cupful tomatoes. Boil at least 2 hours.

MRS. A. WEHMEYER.

Cream of Celery Soup.

1 cup of chopped celery and 1 quart of sweet milk.

Boil 20 minutes; add 1 tablespoonful melted butter and thicken with 2 tablespoonfuls of flour, dissolved in milk or water. Salt and pepper to taste A little cream added improves it.

MRS. HOWARD HONAN.

Fish Chowder.

To every 2 ℔ fish, use 5 medium sized potatoes; 1 large onion; 5 or 6 slices breakfast bacon; canned tomatoes; 2 bay leaves; 1 teaspoonful whole pepper; salt and paprika to taste.

Slice bacon and fry light brown, add potatoes, onion and fish in layers, cover with canned tomatoes into which seasoning has been stirred. Simmer until well done.

Serve as soup, excellent Friday dish.

MRS. H. GOLDSCHMIDT.

MILK SOUP (fine).

1 qt. fresh milk; ¼ qt. water; yolk of 2 eggs; a pinch of salt; whites of 2 eggs beaten stiff; a heaping teaspoonful of sugar; a heaping tablespoonful of cornstarch; lemon peel or vanilla, or 2 fresh peach leaves.

Put on the stove the water and milk, add the cornstarch after it has been dissolved with a little of the water; a pinch of salt and the beaten yolks, also the lemon or peach leaves and sugar, stirring all the time while heating. When it begins to thicken remove from the fire at once and pour into a dish. Drop spoonfuls of the beaten whites of egg on top, and sprinkle with sugar and cinnamon. Then put on cover at once so that the heat may cook the whites.

MRS. O. W. STRIEGLER.

Milk Soup.

½ cup rice; 1 qt. milk; 1 egg; ¼ cup sugar; ½ teaspoon nutmeg.

Cook rice in water until tender. Add milk, then boil a few minutes, take from fire and beat into this 1 egg, add nutmeg. Lastly add the sugar.

MRS. RICHARD HENKE.

Oyster Soup.

2 quarts of milk; yolk of one egg; 1 tablespoonful of butter; 3 small cans of oysters; 1 tablespoonful of flour.

Salt and pepper to taste.

MRS. L. DIETZ.

Pea Soup.

Soak 2 cups of dried peas over night. Next morning cook until half done, then add 1 lb sausage cut into pieces (skin removed), 1 onion, salt and pepper to taste. Keep plenty of water on peas.

MRS. A. WEHMEYER.

Potato Soup with Tomatoes.

Equal parts of potatoes and tomatoes; 1 large onion; and salt to taste.

Boil in sufficient water, until well done, strain through a fine sieve, then add 2 tablespoonfuls of flour, mixed with 2 tablespoonfuls of fresh butter. Add parsley to taste.

MRS. PETER ROEDER.

Peanut Soup.

Grind one cup peanuts, cover with 1 pt. water and simmer 2 hours. Have 1 pt. tomatoes and one onion cut fine; salt, pepper, and a pinch of allspice, 1 teaspoonful sugar and 1 pt. water cooking in another vessel. When ready strain the nut liquid into the other, thicken with flour, and serve.

MRS. HOWARD HONAN.

Cream of Tomato Soup.

1 qt. of tomatoes; 1 qt. of water; 1 qt. of sweet milk; 5 crackers; 2 tablespoonfuls of sugar; 1 teaspoonful of soda; butter and salt.

Cook tomatoes in water until tender. Rub through a sieve. Place tomatoes on the stove and let come to a boil, then add the soda. After it ceases to effervesce, add the boiling milk, rolled crackers, sugar and a little butter and salt. Boil a few minutes. Serve.

MRS. A. H. WELGEHAUSEN.

Cream of Tomato Soup.

1 pt. tomatoes; 1 qt. milk; 1 slice onion; 1 bay leaf; ½ teaspoon soda; 1 tablespoon butter; 1 tablespoon flour; 1 teaspoon sugar; 1 teaspoon salt.

Stew the tomatoes for twenty minutes with the onion and bay leaf, press the tomatoes through a sieve and return to the stove, heat the milk, rub the flour and butter together until smooth, add a little of the hot milk to this mixture, stir until smooth, then add to the remainder of the milk and stir until it thickens to a cream. Add the sugar and salt to the tomatoes, then the soda dissolved in a little cold water; gradually add the milk stirring briskly. The success of this part of the work depends on the milk not curdling. The soup must not be heated after the milk is added.

IDA HENNERSDORF.

Tomato Bisque.

1 quart canned tomatoes, or fresh tomatoes to that amount; 1 quart sweet milk; 1 tablespoonful butter; 1 tablespoonful flour; ¾ teaspoonfuls soda.

Steam the tomatoes and strain. Add the soda to the hot tomatoes and stir. Make a thin paste with the flour and a little of the milk; add to the tomato juice and let come to a boil. Next put in the butter, and last add the remainder of the milk. Season with salt and pepper. Serve with toasted crackers.

MRS. J. T. ESTILL.

Wine Soup.

1 quart of water; ½ cup of sago; ½ cup of wine; a few raisins; vanilla; 1/3 cup of sugar; 2 slices of

lemon; a small piece of stick cinnamon. Toasted bread cubes.

Put a quart of water on the stove to boil. Then add the sago, after it has been rinsed in cold water several times; then the cinnamon, lemons, and raisins. Let this boil until clear and raisins done. Take from the stove and add sugar, wine and vanilla. Just before serving add bread cubes toasted in a little butter. You may add wine and sugar to suit the taste.

MRS O. W. STRIEGLER.

Liver Dumpling Soup.

Wash and boil a good size Soupbone for 2 hours, add a little onion, parsley, salt and pepper to taste. Grind about three or four pieces of liver, two eggs, season with salt and pepper, ½ teaspoon baking powder and enough flour to make a stiff dough. Drop in dumplings by spoon and boil for ½ hour longer.

MRS. A. WALTER.

 # Oysters and Fish

Little Pigs in Blankets.

Take large oysters and around each oyster wrap a thin slice of bacon, securing with wooden tooth picks. Season with salt, pepper, and a little butter. Bake in oven for half hour and serve very hot on toast with celery and garnish the platter with slices of lemon.

MRS. F. L. FREY.

Fish a la Creole.

To a 4 — 5 lb Red fish; 2 ℔ can strained tomatoes; 1 medium size onion; salt and pepper to taste; ¼ ℔ butter; cup soup stock or water; 1 cup cracker crumbs.

Start frying the fish in the butter, cover with crumbs, with onion, tomato and seasoning, bake 45 minutes or 1 hour.

MRS. FRITZ KNUST.

Salmon Croquettes.

1 can salmon; 4 medium sized Irish potatoes; 2 eggs.

After draining the salmon and removing the bones and skins; mix with the potatoes previously boiled and mashed. Add the well-beaten eggs, and pepper and salt to taste. Make out in balls and fry in hot lard. Serve with tomato sauce.

Simmer one-half can tomatoes, one chopped onion, ½ teaspoon salt, ¼ teaspoon pepper, together about ten minutes. Rub through a sieve. Cook together one tablespoon each of flour and butter, and add the tomatoes, gradually cook until as thick as desired.

JULIA ESTILL.

Baked Fish.

After cleaning the fish thoroughly let it stand in salt water for 2 or 3 hours. Rub it well, inside and out, with pepper. Make a dressing of bread crumbs, one tablespoonful of butter, a small onion chopped fine, pepper and salt to taste. Stuff the fish with this dressing and tie or sew up. Put it in a pan with a little water. Sprinkle with flour, adding a small piece of butter. Bake slowly 1 hour. Garnish with hard boiled eggs.

META DIETZ.

Oyster Patties.

Take oysters according to the number to be served and put them in pan with butter, salt, pepper, and a little flour; stir and let simmer for a few minutes.

Bake shells of rich puff paste in patty pans and also rounds for covers; heat the shells and fill with oysters; put on the covers and set in the oven for five minutes. Serve immediately.

MRS. A. L. PATTON.

Salmon Croquettes.

1 can salmon; 2 eggs; salt; Cayenne pepper; bread-crumbs.

Remove bones from salmon, shred with fork, and add salt, Cayenne pepper, and beaten eggs. Into this mix enough fine bread-crumbs to handle well, form into round or oblong shape, roll in cracker crumbs, and fry in hot lard.

MRS. A. L. PATTON.

Fish Premier with Premier Sauce.

4 ℔ fish; salt and pepper; 2 doz. large oysters; ¼ cup butter; yolk of 1 egg; juice of ½ lemon remove the head and tail of fish, skin and bone it, leaving two oblong pieces. Lay one of the pieces on a greased baking sheet in the baking pan, cover with half the oysters. Sprinkle thickly with the crumbs and pour over them one-half of the meited butter. Then, cover it with the other half of the fish. Place the remaining oysters on top of that piece of fish, sprinkle with salt and pepper. Place the rest of the crumbs on the oysters and pour the remaining butter over the crumbs. Put into a moderate oven and brown. When done slip it carefully into a hot platter, garnish with watercress and sliced lemon. Serve with the following sauce:

¼ cup butter; yolk of 1 egg; juice of ½ lemon; ¼ teaspoon salt; 1/3 cup boiling water; pinch of white pepper.

Cook in double boiler for six minutes and serve in a separate bowl. Sufficient for six persons. Delicious.

MRS. F. L. FREY.

Fried Oysters.

Select fresh good sized oysters. Pick them up by the muscular portion of the oyster and place them on a dry board. Dry them carefully with a soft cheese cloth. Sprinkle with salt. To each dozen oysters allow 1 egg. Beat the white and yolk together until thoroughly mixed; add a tablespoon of warm water;

beat again. Turn oysters in nicely rolled and dried bread crumbs, then quickly into the egg and back into the bread crumbs. Fry in oil or lard 360° (Fahr.); when golden brown lift out and drain on paper. Do not prick oyster with a fork. Serve at once.

MRS. VICTOR KEIDEL.

Oyster Salad.

Drain the liguid from a quart of fresh oysters. Put them in hot vinegar, enough to cover, place over hot fire. Let them remain until plump, but not cooked, then drop them immediately in cold water, drain off, and mix with them two pickled cucumbers cut fine, also a quart of celery cut in dice pieces, some seasoning of salt and pepper. Mix well with wooden spoon or silver fork. Pour over the whole a Mayonnaise dressing. Garnish with celery tips.

MRS. GEO. E. KOTT.

Escalloped Fish.

Two cups left over fish, picked over and freed of bones. 1 cup thin white sauce, bread crumbs. Butter a baking dish and line with crumbs. Add a layer of fish, using half, and cover with half the sauce. Cover with a layer of crumbs. Add another layer of fish. sauce and crumbs, making this last layer of crumbs quite thick. Place in a hot oven and leave until crumbs are brown and fish is heated through.

VERDIE KETTNER.

Fried Oysters.

1 pint large oysters; ½ cup milk; ½ cup tomato catsup; ½ teaspoon salt; ½ cup flour; mix thoroughly

flour, milk, catsup and salt; dip oysters into mixture, then roll them in cracker crumbs.

Fry in sweet, fresh lard, butter or olive oil until a dark brown. Serve very hot.

MRS. MAX WINKEL.

Salmon Loaf.

Mix 1 can salmon from which bones and skin have been removed, with 1 cup cracker crumbs, and 2 well beaten eggs. Make sauce by browning 2 tablespoons butter; add 2 tablespoons flour, then add 3 thinly sliced green peppers, 2 cups sliced tomatoes with juice add a pinch of salt to tomatoes. Add salt and pepper. Let cook until pepper and tomatoes are soft, then add 2 cups milk. Put layer of salmon in well greased baking dish and cover with sauce then another layer salmon and finish top with sauce. **Bake** ½ hour.

ELLA EVERS.

Fish Sauce.

½ teaspoon parsley; 1 teaspoon butter; 1 teaspoon flour; ½ pint soup stock; 4 tablespoons capers; 1 teaspoon salt; 1 teaspoon Chili Powder. Heat butter, add flour, stock, boil 10 minutes, add capers, when nearly done.

MRS. HARRY HEYLAND.

Fried Oysters
Done in Oven With Tarter Sauce.

Roll the required number of oysters in flour, season with salt and pepper, dip in beaten egg, then roll in vegetable oil. Bake in hot oven until a light brown. Serve with tartar sauce, which is made by adding chopped olives, parsley and capers to Mayonnaise dressing.

MRS. HARRY HEYLAND.

 # Poultry and Game

Chicken Curry.

Cut up a chicken weighing from 1½ to 2 pounds, as for fricassee. Wash it well, put into a stewpan with sufficient water to cover it, boil closely covered until tender, add a large teaspoonful of salt and cook a few minutes longer. Remove from the fire, take out the chicken, pour the liquid into a bowl and set it aside.

Now cut up into the stew pan two small onions and fry them with a piece of butter, size of an egg. As soon as they are brown skim them out and put in the chicken, fry for three or four minutes. Next sprinkle over the chicken two teaspoonfuls of Curry Powder. Now pour over the liquid in which the chicken was stewed, stir all well together and stew for five minutes longer. Then stir into this a tablespoonful of sifted flour mixed with a little water. Lastly stir in a beaten yolk of egg and it is done. Serve with hot boiled rice laid around on the edge of a platter and the chicken curry in the center.

MRS. F. L. FREY.

Jellied Chicken.

1 chicken; 1 onion; 2 bay leaves; ½ teaspoonful of white pepper; 1 teaspoonful of salt; 3 cloves; ½ box of powdered gelatine.

Singe and draw chicken, place in a kettle of boiling water, boil until tender. Lift the chicken out and set aside to cool. Then cut into neat pieces. Take one quart of the liquid in which the chicken was boiled and add the onion, bay leaves, pepper, salt, cloves and boil for five minutes. Then add the gelatine (which has been dissolved) and strain. Arrange the chicken in a wet mould, fill with the stock. Place on ice to jell. Serve with mayonnaise dressing.

MRS. A. H. WELGEHAUSEN.

Chicken Dumplings.

Disjoint the fowl and cook in about 2 quarts of water till tender, season with salt, whole peppers, whole cloves, (and if desired a little nutmeg). Make thick batter for dumplings as follows:

1 pint flour; 2 teaspoonfuls baking powder; ½ teaspoonful salt; 2 eggs; enough sweet milk to make stiff batter.

Drop by tablespoonfuls in boiling liquid on top of chicken and boil from 15 to 20 minutes.

MRS. ARNOLD KOTT.

Dressing for Turkey.

Bread; fresh pork; 3 eggs; giblets; 1 tablespoonful of ginger; salt.

Take bread enough to fill turkey and pour boiling milk or water over it. When thoroughly soaked, place in a muslin bag, squeeze carefully until dry. Then add ½ lb of fresh pork and giblets chopped fine, three or four eggs well beaten, one tablespoonful of ginger. Salt to taste. Mix well. This dressing should be as light as bread after it is cooked.

MRS. F. STEIN.

Chicken a la King.

2 cupfuls diced chickenmeat (white preferred); 6 tablespoonfuls chopped green peppers; ½ teaspoonful salt; 3 cupfuls rich cream; 1 tablespoonful butter; 5 tablespoonfuls olive oil; 3 tablespoonfuls chopped pimentoes; 1 tablespoonful capers; 1 can or 1½ cupfuls fresh mushrooms; 2¼ tablespoonfuls flour; 2 egg-yolks; paprika.

Cook mushrooms five minutes in the olive oil, then add the mixture ot the chicken, capers, peppers and pimentoes, and add a dash of paprika and salt. Prepare a white sauce of the butter, flour and cream, beating the two egg-yolks and pouring the sauce into them when it is done. Add the chicken mixture, heat thoroughly and serve either in individual ramekins or patti cases, or on diamond-shaped slices of buttered toast.   **MARY LOVE.**

Haunch of Venison (baked).

Allow all game to air from 48 to 60 hours. Lard well with bacon that has been turned in salt and pepper.

Rub haunch well with salt and pepper. Heat bacon, grease and butter in large covered baking-pan. Bake basting frequently. Add hot water or soup stock gradually. 10 minutes before serving add ¼ cup thick sour cream. If necessary thicken with small amount of corn starch.

MRS. FRITZ KNUST.

Pressed Chicken.

Cut up the fowls and place in a kettle with a light cover so as to retain the steam. Add enough water to cover and salt and pepper to taste. Allow it to cook until the meat drops easily from the bones. Chop fine, add a little allspice, put in a dish and press, pour over it the remainder of the stock in which it was cooked. Set in a cool place until jellied.

MAYONNAISE DRESSING FOR PRESSED CHICKEN.

3 eggs well beaten; ½ cup of sugar; ½ teaspoonful salt; a pinch of Cayenne pepper; ½ teaspoonful black pepper; ½ teaspoonful mustard; 1 tablespoonful olive oil; 1 tablespoonful butter; 1 cup of vinegar.

Boil until thick.

MRS. LOUIS DIETZ.

Stuffing,
like Mother used to make!

Light bread; ½ cup currants; ½ cup nuts; 1 cup sliced apples; liver, gizzard and heart of fowls chopped finely; 2 eggs; salt and pepper.

Soak a sufficient quantity of light bread, wring dry, add enough milk or cream to handle well with mixing spoon. Turn in currants, apples, nuts and the meat that has been previously fried in butter with a suggestion of onion. Mix in yolks of eggs and seasoning, add beaten whites and stuff fowls with the mixture.

Excellent especially for game.

MRS. H. GOLDSCHMIDT.

Chicken or Turkey Dressing.

Gizzard, heart and liver of fowl; 4 of 5 slices of bread; 4 eggs; 1 medium-sized onion; 2 tablespoonfuls flour; pepper and salt to taste, also a little nutmeg if liked.

Take heart and gizzard and boil ½ hour adding a pinch of salt. Soak bread in water, squeeze out and add eggs to it. Chop fine the heart, gizzard and raw liver with onion. Mix with bread and eggs, using the water in which the heart and gizzard were boiled in mixing. To this add flour, pepper and salt. Mix all together using enough milk to make a soft dough.

Melt a heaping tablespoonful of butter, when hot enough pour in dressing. Fry until brown then cut crosswise and turn. When half done pour over a sufficient quantity of chicken gravy at different times, cover and fry slowly.

MRS. FRED. WALTER.

Roast Quail.

Put 2 tablespoons butter in each of the birds to prevent their getting dry. Slit 2 pieces of bacon once or twice and tie over breasts of birds which should be trussed for roasting. Wrap in buttered paper and bake in a quick oven 30 minutes, basting well and frequently. For the last 8 minutes remove paper and bacon, sprinkle with a little flour, salt, and pepper, baste well and brown. Serve on a hot dish garnished with rolls of bacon. Hand with it gravy, bread sauce, and guava jelly.

MISS ZULA MAE HILL.

Chicken Fricassee.

Put a chicken, cut into joints, in enough boiling water to cover, add salt and let simmer slowly until tender. Melt 2 tablespoons of butter; add flour, then the chicken stock, a little nutmeg and the yolks of 2 eggs just before serving.

Ribs of a young calf can be prepared the same way.

MRS. VICTOR KEIDEL.

Turkey Dressing.

½ loaf stale light bread; 1 cake of corn bread; 6 boiled eggs; ½ pound butter; 1 good sized onion if desired, and pepper and salt to taste.

Boil neck and gizzard of the turkey and take the juice to make up the dressing then add a good sized potato.

MRS. R. C. LUDWIG.

Turkey Dressing.

1 lb ground meat; 1 grated raw potato; 1 onion; 1 green pepper; ½ can Chili and Rice; 1 tablespoon flour; 2 slices cornbread; 2 eggs; a little sweet cream, pepper and salt.

MRS. JOHN OSTROW.

MEATS

Beef Loaf with Tomatoes.

3 lb chopped beef; ½ lb chopped pork; 1 large onion; 1 pint jar or can of tomatoes; 1 large cup of bread crumbs; butter the size of an egg.

Chop onion fine; add to chopped meat and bread which has been soaked in cold water. Mix all together with tomatoes and season with pepper and salt. Bake in loaf pan about one hour.

BELLE STEBBINS.

Beef Loaf.

2 lb of raw beef ground fine; ¼ lb of salt pork; 3 eggs; ¾ cup cracker crumbs; 1 tablespoon melted butter; salt and pepper to taste; onion if liked.

Mold in loaf, grate crackers over top and bake.

MRS. A. W. MOURSUND.

Boneless Birds.

1½ lb round steak; 3 slices bacon; 1 grated onion; 1 pint boiling water; 3 tablespoons butter or drippings; 1 tablespoon browned flour, salt and pepper.

Cut steak in four inch pieces. Lay on each a small piece of bacon and onion, roll up, and tie with string, or use tooth-picks. Brown and put in pan with gravy made with flour, butter, and water. Cook slowly one hour.

MRS. A. W. MOURSUND.
MRS. W. J. JUNG.

Cabbage Stuffed with Meat.

8 oz. ground beef; 3 to 4 oz. oz soaked bread; 2½ oz. butter; 2 eggs; salt, nutmeg and pepper.

Mix these ingredients and form into balls. Then take large leaves of cabbage which have been scalded with boiling water and cut out the hard veins. Cover meat balls with cabbage leaves and tie together with thread. Then boil 1 hour adding 1 cup of water, some butter and nutmeg, take out cabbage balls and add a little flour to the gravy and pour over the balls.

MRS. O. W. STRIEGLER.

Mutton Stew.

2 lb mutton chops; 2 tablespoonfuls flour; lard, water, allspice; cloves, pepper and salt; a few bay leaves and one onion.

Fry chops in lard until brown. Remove from pan, then add wtaer, flour, and seasoning, and cook to smooth gravy. Pour over chops and serve at once.

MRS. RICHARD HENKE.

Stuffed Green Peppers.

Cut off tops of sweet green peppers, remove seeds. Take equal parts of cold chopped meat and slightly moistened bread crumbs. Season with finely chopped tomato, add salt and pepper to taste as well as a generous piece of butter. Fill peppers, place in a pan with a little water and butter. Bake slowly until done.

MRS. TEMPLE D. SMITH.

Meat Loaf.

1 lb lean beef; ½ lb pork or mutton; 1 cup of bread crumbs; 2 green peppers, chopped up; 1 onion; 1 egg; 1 tablespoonful salt.

Grind up the meat, mix in salt, peppers, bread crumbs, onion and egg. Cover with the following sauce.

2 cups tomato juice; 2 tablespoonfuls corn starch; 4 tablespoonfuls shortening; 1 tablespoonful salt.

Bake one hour. This recipe is sufficient for six people.

MRS. OTTO EVERS.

Meat Olives.

Flank steaks; bacon (sliced); onion, chopped; ½ cup toasted bread crumbs; salt and pepper to taste.

Split steaks lengthwise, cut into pieces 5x3 in., place slice of bacon and onion on each, season to taste, sprinkle with crumbs, roll up and tie with thread or skewer with tooth picks.

Brown meat rolls in half lard and half fat, cover with boiling soup stock or water and simmer over slow fire an hour and a half. The meat must be tender and the gravy rich and brown.

MRS. H. F. RANSLEBEN.

A Good Steak.

1 ℔ of steak; 1 egg; flour; pepper and salt.

One pound of steak seasoned with pepper and salt. Dip in well beaten egg, then in flour and fry at once in hot lard and butter mixed to a light brown.

MRS. F. STEIN.

Scalloped Sweetbreads.

Soak sweetbreads in salt water for half an hour. Boil until well done, then remove skins and small pipes and cut into small pieces. Into a buttered pudding dish put a layer of rolled crackers, then a layer of sweetbreads until dish is full, add salt and pepper. Strain the water the sweetbreads were boiled in, add milk to make enough liquid to cover the crackers and sweetbreads. Dot with bits of butter and bake in a hot oven until a nice brown.

MRS. A. WEHMEYER.

Planked Steak.

Have choice sirloin steak cut almost two inches thick, and cut through edge to prevent curling. Heat oven eight or ten minutes, and set plank in upper oven to heat, while meat is broiling beneath flame. Brown steak quickly on each side, then reduce flame and finish cooking more slowly. Place meat on the plank, season well with salt, pepper, butter creamed with lemon juice, and minced parsley, garnish with potato border and small stuffed tomatoes pimentoes or green peppers and cress. Serve piping hot.

MRS. FELIX W. MAIER.

Pickled Meat.

2 ℔ of yellow sugar; 5 ℔ of salt; 4 oz. of saltpeter; 14 quarts of water.

Cook slowly, until briné will carry an egg. When cold, pour the brine over the meat.

MRS. WM. WEYRICH.

Sliced Tongue.

Boil the tongue in about 2 quarts of water until tender. Remove from liquid, skin and cut into slices, melt ½ tablespoon of butter in a pan, add half an onion and fry over slow fire until yellow. Add the boiling liquid and season with salt, pepper, juice of one lemon, half a tablespoon of sugar or more, and half a teaspoon of flour mixed with a little water. Now add the sliced tongue and boil from 15 to 20 minutes.

MRS. ARNOLD KOTT.

Veal Loaf.

3 ℔ of veal; seasonings; and gelatine.

Boil 3 pounds of lean veal in enough water to cover it well. Add a little salt, and boil slowly, until the meat falls from the bones. Take out the meat and set aside to cool. To the liquid in which the meat was cooked, add pepper and salt to taste, a few cloves, two bay leaves, a little celery salt or seed, a few mustard seeds and the grated rind of a lemon. Cook the liquid about ½ hour longer with the seasoning, then add 2 tablespoonfuls of gelatine, (dissolved in a little cold water), and strain. Arrange the chopped meat in a wet mold, and pour the liquid over it. Let stand until the next day, when it may be turned out on a flat dish and sliced. When serving garnish with parsley and sliced lemon or sliced tomatoes.

MRS. R. G. STRIEGLER.

White Fricassee of Tongue.

Tongue boiled in salt water, diced fine. Melt a sufficient quantity of butter browned slightly, one chopped onion and a tablespoon flour, add the boiled down liquid from the tongue. Add slices of lemon, from which the seed have been carefully removed, mace white pepper to taste and ½ glass white wine and put the diced tongue into the liquid, boiling both together over a very slow fire. Serve with small round meat dumplings that have been boiled in salt water or soup stock. The sauce may be thickened with the yolks of eggs before serving which greatly improves both taste and appearance.

MRS. F. MORGAN.

Pickled Meat.

To 100 ℔ meat, allow 8 ℔ salt; ¾ ℔ sugar (Kandis-Zucker); 2 oz. saltpeter; 32 quarts water.

Boil and then allow to cool.

The meat, cut, is placed into the barrel or crock; the cooled brine poured over. Small boards weighted with stones laid on top to keep meat well under brine. The pieces reserved for smoking should be removed after two weeks while the rest may remain in pickle until used. From time to time pieces of beef or tongue may be placed in same brine without detriment to taste.

MRS. BANNOWSKY.

Lambs Chops with Green Peppers.

4 large lamb chops, 1½ cupfuls stock, 2 small onions, minced 1 teaspoon curry-powder, 2 green peppers, chopped, 1½ tablespoon corn flour, 1 cupful canned tomatoes, salt and pepper.

(Cut chops from leg of lamb; 4 chops will weigh about 1½ ℔).

Fry the onions and chopped peppers in three (3) tablespoons of lamb fat, until tender. Add the tomatoes, stock and seasonings to taste. Thicken with flour mixed with a little cold water. Broil chops slightly, season, lay them in a baking dish, pour over the sauce, and bake ten minutes in a hot oven. Serve with rice timbles. The above recipe will serve four.

MRS. ALFRED P. C. PETSCH.

Curry Salad Dressing.

½ teaspoon curry powder, 1 tablespoon tarragon vinegar or lemon juice, 6 tablespoons olive oil or salad oil, ½ teaspoon onion salt, ¼ teaspoon pepper.

Mix thoroughly all dry ingredients and oil, add slowly the the vinegar to thin. This is especially good with cold fish.

MRS. ALFRED P. C. PETSCH.

French Steak.

Take a flank steak, remove the fat and score the steak by cutting lightly crosswise with knife. Put a piece of fat in one end and roll the steak, fastening with sticks an inch apart. Then cut in inch slices, leaving a stick in each slice. Have broiler hot and greased. Sear one side and then the other. Let cook twenty-five minutes. Sprinkle with salt, pepper, and melted butter. Serve with parsley garnishments.

MRS. WILLIE MARSCHAL.

Swiss Steak.

1 round steak 1½ or 2 inches thick, 1 small can of tomatoes, 1 onion, a little flour, salt and pepper.

Take the steak and beat it thoroughly with a plate, then sift flour over steak and beat it in, then chop an onion fine and beat it in well, add salt and pepper. Put steak in a pan containing a tablespoon of hot lard, place in a moderate oven and bake for three quarters of an hour, remove from the oven and pour over the steak a can of tomatoes, add more salt and pepper and put back in the oven and let brown a little more, then serve at once. The juice of the meat and tomatoes makes a delicious sauce.

MRS. HARRY M. HARRINGTON.

Tamale Loaf.

Two ℔ ground beef; 3 cups of corn meal; 2|3 cup of lard; 3 tablespoons of flour; 1/3 cup of garlic; 2 teaspoonfuls of commino seed; 3 tablespoonfuls of powdered chili pepper; 2 quarts of water; salt to taste.

Pour one cup of boiling water over commino seed and set aside to steep. Put lard in stew-pan, when hot add the ground meat, stir until it begins to brown, then add flour to thicken, chili pepper, salt, garlic, and the water from the commino seed, then add two quarts of plain boiling water, cover and let boil for two hours. Then add enough boiling water to corn meal (to which has been added teaspoonful of salt) to make a thick paste. Put a layer of this paste into a baking dish, then a layer of the meat, then a layer of the meal paste and so on until dish is filled to about two inches of the top, lastly pour some of the chili sauce over the top, saving some of the sauce to serve with the loaf, put dish in oven and bake about twenty minutes. Serve at once.

MRS. HARRY M. HARRINGTON.

Turkish Tongue.

1 fresh beef tongue; ½ ℔ raisins; ½ lb dates; 1 carrot; 1 sweet pepper; 1 teaspoon salt; 1 onion; 4 tablespoons butter.

Wash tongue, cover with boiling water and cook slowly for 2 hours. Skin and tie in shape. Put lump of butter into the kettle, add pepper, chopped onions, and peeled carrot, cut in fancy shape. Shake this over fire, until slightly brown. Put in tongue, raisins, and dates; add one quart of the water in which the tongue was boiled. Cover and simmer gently 2 hours longer. Serve tongue in center of dish with vegetables and fruit around it.

MRS. WM. KUENEMANN.

Tamale Pie.

2 cups corn meal; 2½ teaspoon salt; 6 cups boiling water. Cook a good stiff mush, line your pan and keep enough to put on a top crust.

FILLING: 2 good sized onions; 1 ℔ hamburger steak; 2 cups tomatoes; 3 teaspoons chili powder; 4 green peppers.

Brown onions in lard, add meat, fry until red color disappears, add tomatoes, pepper, salt and chili powder. Bake 40 minutes or till brown.

MRS. ALBERT KOENNECKE.

Beafsteak Pie.

¾ ℔ round flank steak, cut in small pieces of uniform size; 1 tablespoonful flour; 3 cupfuls hot water; ¼ teaspoonful pepper; 1 teaspoonful salt; 10 small onions; 3 medium-sized potatoes, diced.

CRUST: 1 cupful flour; 1½ teaspoonfuls baking powder; ¼ teaspoonful salt; 1 tablespoonful fat; ¼ cupful milk.

Remove the fat from the meat and fry out. Sprinkle meat with flour and brown in fat and cook till partially done. Add the seasonings, onions, potatoes, and hot water. Continue to cook in covered fryingpan or put into a bakingdish, cover, and cook slowly until the meat is done. Make a crust of the above ingredients. Roll into one sheet large enough for top of pie. Bake 15 minutes in a hot oven.

MRS. VIDA G. NEWBERRY.

Veal Roast with Tomatoes.
A famous Southern Dish.

Wash a fresh tender roast of veal weighing about 4 ℔. Lard it well and sprinkle with 2 teaspoons salt and ½ teaspoon pepper. Dredge with flour on both sides; lay in a rather small deep baking pan with boiling water enough to nearly cover it and roast for 1 hour, basting with gravy every ten minutes . Then turn on other side and spread over the roast 1 pint of tomatoes, peeled and sliced, 2 onions, 2 sprigs parsley chopped fine, and two or three whole green peppers. Baste for another hour every 10 minutes, add boiling water if needed. Serve hot with its own gravy of which there should be 1 pint.

MRS. O. B. WITTE.

MACARONI, RICE, PANCAKES, EGGS, POTATOES, ETC.

Cheese Soufflee.

1 cupful of cheese; 3 tablespoonfuls of flour; ½ cupful of sweet milk; 1 cupful of hot milk; 4 eggs; ½ teaspoonful salt; dash of pepper.

Mix the flour and cold milk well; add this to the hot milk and cook until thick, add cheese, stir until cheese melts. Add yolks of eggs well beaten; remove from fire, add salt, a dash of pepper. Stir in carefully the whites well beaten. Bake in a moderate oven.

MRS. A. B. WILLIAMSON.

Cheese Corn Soufflee.

1 cupful grated cheese; 1 cupful canned corn; 3 eggs; 1 tablespoonful butter; 1 tablespoonful of flour; 1 cup sweet milk.

Cook together the butter and flour; pour upon it the milk and stir until smooth and thickened; add the cheese, and when this is blended, add the corn, chopped or ground and drained from the liquid. Put in the weel-beaten yolks of the eggs; season with salt and pepper and add the stiffly beaten whites of the eggs. Bake in a buttered dish in a moderate oven for half an hour.

MRS. J. T. ESTILL.

Ham Soufflee.

1 cup of cold chopped ham; ½ cup of bread crumbs; 1 small onion, a bit of parsley cut fine.

Pepper, salt to suit taste. Beat 3 eggs, adding 1 pint of milk, mix all together. Bake 25 minutes. Serve with tomato sauce.

MISS META DIETZ.

Stuffed Eggs.

One dozen hard boiled eggs; one-half teaspoonful of mustard; two heaping tablespoonfuls of cold boiled ham or chicken; one tablespoonful of butter; one tablespoonful of pickles; salt and pepper to taste.

Remove the shells and cut lengthwise, take out yolks and rub to a smooth paste with the mustard and butter, then add the ham or meat, salt and pepper and mix thoroughly. Fill the hollowed whites with this mixture.

MRS. A. H. WELGEHAUSEN.

Macaroni and Cheese.

Break 1 box of macaroni into small pieces, put in well salted boiling water and boil 20 to 25 minutes stirring frequently. When done drain, add 2 tablespoonfuls butter, 3 oz. grated cheese and enough milk to about cover, mix well and heat; then pour into a buttered dish, sprinkle a layer of cheese on top and bake for about ½ hour. Serve at once.

MRS. A. WEHMEYER.

Spanish Macaroni.

2 slices bacon; 1 pint macaroni; 1 pint stewed tomatoes; 1 cup cold cooked meat; 1 or 2 onions; 1 green sweet pepper; butter to grease pan; milk or soup stock.

Fry onions, bacon and pepper. Fill pan a layer of macaroni and a layer of tomatoes mixed with the other ingredients.

MRS. A. W. MOURSUND.

Mexican Rice.

1 cup rice; 2 tablespoons butter or lard; 1 tablespoon chili powder; ½ cup chopped tomatoes; 1 tablespoon minced onion; salt to taste.

Put butter or lard in a skillet, add the well washed rice and brown, stirring to prevent burning. When brown add the onion, tomato, chili powder and salt. Then add boiling water enough to cook the rice thoroughly.

MRS. HOWARD HONAN.

Mexican Rice (sopa seca.)

1 teaspoon lard; 1 cup rice; 4 tomatoes, medium size; salt; Cayenne; onion juice to taste.

Heat to the smoking point a heaping teaspoon of lard, throw in rice (dry) and stir while it browns gently. Have tomatoes ready peeled and cut, add these quickly with the seasoning, stir until tomatoes soften, add enough water to swell rice and cook until soft on a slow fire.

Serve with chili and beans, or fried sausage.

MRS. HERM. GOLDSCHMIDT.

Quick Rice.

To 1 cup of washed rice add 4 cups boiling water and 1 teaspoon salt. Put in pan and bake in oven 40 minutes.

MRS. HOWARD HONAN.

Browned Rice with Chili.

Wash ½ cup of rice and lay on cloth to dry, then melt 2 tablespoonfuls of butter, put the rice in stirring constantly until a nice brown, pour over enough water to cover well, and let simmer until soft, adding ½ teaspoon of salt and 1 teaspoon of chili powder.

MRS. D. A. RILEY.

German Milk Rice.

1 cup washed rice; 6 times quantity water; 1 pt. rich milk; ½ cup sugar; 1 tablespoon butter; 2 yolks of eggs.

Boil rice until tender but grains are still whole, drain off water, add milk, sugar and butter. When done, remove from fire, and carefully beat in yolks of eggs. Turn into dish and sprinkle liberally with sugar and cinnamon.

MRS. H. F. RANSLEBEN.

Potato Balls.

2 cups mashed potatoes; 1 teaspoon butter; 3 yolks of eggs; ½ cup of milk; 2 heaping tablespoons of flour.

Mix ingredients into a soft but firm dough, scoop up with teaspoon, drop into deep fat and brown slowly and evenly. Very fine.

MRS. H. F. RANSLEBEN.

Pan Cakes.

1 cup of meal; 1 cup of flour; a pinch of salt; 1 cup of sour milk; ¾ teaspoon of soda; 2 well beaten eggs.

Sift together corn meal, flour and salt. Then add milk to which soda has been added and lastly the eggs well beaten.

MRS. O. W. STRIEGLER.

Hot Cakes.

Take ¼ of an yeast cake, enough water and flour to make a soft sponge, let this rise over night. When ready to use, add 2 cups flour, 2 eggs, 2 cups milk. Beat well, and fry in hot lard.

MRS. JOHN OSTROW.

First Class Pan Cake.

2 eggs, 1 tablespoon of flour, ½ cup milk, a pinch of salt.

Beat eggs 10 minutes, slowly add the flour, then the milk and salt. Heat a little butter and lard in a frying pan, drop batter in, and set in oven for half an hour. Sprinkle thickly with sugar and serve.

MRS. JOHN OSTROW.

Pilau.

Boil a cupful of rice in a pint of mutton-stock which has been skimmed and seasoned with onion, tomato, salt and cayenne. When the rice is soft and has soaked up all the liquid add a tablespoonful of butter.

Mince cold mutton or lamb until you have a cupful; heat a cupful of gravy, season well and thicken with browned flour, then stir in the minced meat, and boil up once. Pour upon a heated platter and arrange the rice like a fence around it. Pilau is even better when made with chicken-stock and meat instead of mutton.

MRS. OTTO KOLMEIER.

Potato Croquettes.

Boil 6 large potatoes in salt water, mash and mix in the yolk of one egg and a litte parsley, make into cone shape, beat the white of an egg, first roll cones in egg and then roll in brown bread crumbs, fry in butter until nicely browned.

MRS. H. CORDES.

Potato Dumplings.
(Rohe Kartoffel-Kloesse.)

5 or 6 medium sized potatoes grated and pressed fairly dry; the mass is then moistened with boiling milk and made into a dough not too thin but yet not firm enough to form into balls. Add salt to taste and mix in bread croutons cut into cubes. Drop by spoonfuls into boiling salt-water and allow half an hour after the last one is in. Remove from water carefully without breaking and serve at once.

MRS. CLARA BITTNER.

Potato Dumplings.

Cream butter the size of a large walnut, add the yolks of two eggs, one saucer full of bread crumbs, one saucer full of grated boiled potatoes (which should not be watery), lemon peeling, nutmeg and salt, and lastly the stiffly beaten whites of the eggs. Drop by small spoonfuls, into boiling water, and boil about 10 minutes.

MRS. HILMAR WEBER.

Stuffed Potatoes.

Bake 7 good sized potatoes. When done, cut off a lengthwise slice; scoop out potatoes with a spoon, then mash. Add 1 tablespoon butter, salt and pepper to taste; ½ cupful milk, and the beaten whites of 2 eggs. Refill skins with this mixture. Pile lightly and bake until potatoes are puffed and brown.

MRS. FELIX KLAERNER.

 Vegetables

Asparagus.

Scrape the stems of the asparagus lightly but very clean, throw them into cold water as soon as scraped; tie into bunches of equal size, and drop into plenty of boiling water, well salted. It usually cooks in 20 or 30 minutes. In a saucepan, mix a tablespoonful of slightly browned flour, with a large spoonful of butter, add enough of the liquid in which the asparagus was boiled to make a thick sauce, add salt and pepper to taste and two tablespoonfuls of sweet cream. Add the asparagus, and let simmer a minute, when it is ready to serve.

MRS. R. G. STRIEGLER.

Asparagus Parfoit.

1 bunch asparagus; 1 pint green peas; 4 eggs; seasoning; about 1 pint Golden Sauce.

Cut asparagus, after removing the tough portions, into 1 inch length, and cook until tender. Also cook peas, and hard cook the eggs, which should then be sliced. Combine lightly the asparagus and peas and season with 1 teaspoon salt. Place on a hot platter, and pour over the Golden Sauce made while the vegetables are cooking. Garnish with hard cooked eggs, and small toast points, on each of which place a narrow strip of green or red sweet pepper radiating outward.

GOLDEN SAUCE.

Melt in a sauce pan 2 tablespoons of butter, add 2 tablespoons flour, and cook until bubbling. Add gradually 1 pint milk. Cook until smooth and thickened; then season with 1½ teaspoon salt, ¼ teaspoon pepper, and a dash of cayenne pepper. Remove from stove, and add well beaten yolk of 1 egg, stirring rapidly.

MRS. ALFRED P. C. PETSCH.

Cucumbers.

Remove the seed of 4 large cucumbers, cut into dice and cook about ¾ hour in ½ cup water, ¾ cup vinegar and ½ cup sugar. Squash may be cooked the same way.

MRS. HILMAR WEBER.

Fried Cauliflower.

Boil the cauliflower until half done. Mix two tablespoonfuls of flour with the yolks of two eggs, then add water enough to make a thin paste. Add salt to taste and two well beaten whites of eggs. Dip each branch of cauliflower into the mixture, and fry in hot lard. When done, take out with a skimmer, turn into a colander, dust with salt, and serve hot.

MRS. JOE STEIN.

Celery Croquettes.

Mince the white part of the celery and mix well with an equal quantity of bread crumbs; to a quart of the mixture add the yolks of 2 eggs, a heaping teaspoonful of salt, and a pinch of cayenne; if the moisture from the celery is not sufficient, add a little milk. Shape in cones, dip in egg and crumbs and fry in hot lard.

MRS. B. L. ENDERLE.

Stewed Carrots.

1 qt. of carrots; 1 cupful of onion; salt and butter

Scrape carrots and cut into small squares enough for one quart; cook in salt water until tender. Drain. Soak, one small cupful of onion cut fine, in salt water, for ten minutes. Drain. Fry onions in two large tablespoonfuls of butter to a light brown, add small tablespoonful of flour, mix with carrots and cook for ten minutes.

MRS. F. STEIN.

Baked Cabbage.

Drop well-washed cabbage leaf by leaf into boiling water and boil 20 minutes, adding a tablespoon of salt to a quart of water.

Drain. chop finely, arrange in a baking dish, add a cup of bread crumbs and a sauce made of milk thickened with corn starch and a piece of butter.

Bake 15 minutes.

MRS. O. EVERS.

Filled Cabbage.

Take a small head of cabbage, cut fine, boil tender in salt water, drain; add 3 well-beaten eggs, pepper, salt, a small onion and 2 cups soaked light bread. If too thin, add flour. Place this in a cabbage leaf, tie in a white rag and boil in salt water for 1 hour.

Serve with browned butter.

MRS. L. HENZE.

Creamed Cabbage.

Chop cabbage to make two quarts. Cover with cold water, soak one hour; drain; cover with boiling water, 1 teaspoonful of salt; boil for twenty minutes, uncovered; drain again. Rub together 1 tablespoonful of butter and 1 tablespoonful of flour, add ½ pint of milk; stir until it boils. Season with a teaspoonful of salt and pepper, add the cabbage, heat carefully, and serve.

MISS ALMA SCHUCH.

Baked Green Corn.

To two cups of cooked green corn cut from cob and chopped fine, add 2 eggs slightly beaten, one teaspoon salt, ⅛ teaspoon of pepper, 1 teaspoon of sugar, 2 tablespoons melted butter and 2 cups of scalded milk.

Mix well and turn into buttered pudding dish. Bake until firm, in moderate oven.

MRS. G. L. STEBBINS.

Broiled Egg-Plant.

Peel and cut into rather thin slices and lay in salted ice-water for an hour; spread upon a soft towel and cover with another, patting and pressing the slices until they are entirely dry. Leave them for 10 minutes in a mixture of three tablespoonfuls of olive oil and the juice of half a lemon; sprinkle then with salt and pepper, and broil quickly upon a wire broiler. Twelve minntes should cook both sides.

MRS. AD. CRENWELGE.

Stuffed Peppers.

4 sweet green peppers; 1 cup cooked rice; 1 cup cold minced chicken; 2 tablespoons finely cut celery; onion juice; pepper and salt; 2 tablespoons melted butter; ½ cup tomatoes.

Split peppers in half, remove seeds and ribs. Mix the ingredients, fill into peppers, grate cheese over top and bake in pan with little water.

MRS. A. W. MOURSUND.

Stuffed Egg-Plant.

Parboil a good sized egg-plant for about 10 minutes, and throw at once into cold salted water. Leave there for an hour. Cut into halves, lengthwise, and scoop out seeds and pulp, leaving the walls half an inch thick. Run the pulp through a food-chopper; add to it about a cup of minced chicken (or any kind of meat). Add salt and pepper and ½ cupful of fine dry bread crumbs. Fill the halves with this stuffing and tie together with a string. Put into a baking-dish with two tablespoonfuls of water and butter, or the same of stock; cover closely and bake in a moderate oven for half an hour. Remove the string and serve.

MRS. WM. CRENWELGE.

Goulash.

3 large onions; 1 can tomatoes; 1 teaspoon paprika; 8 medium sized potatoes; 1 coffeespoon salt; 2 lb rump steak.

Chop onions and brown in lard or a good-sized piece of bacon, add paprika and salt and when well thinned, add the meat cut into small pieces. Let this fry to a crisp and light brown in color, add 3 large tomatoes or a pound of canned. Simmer slowly until half done, then add potatoes cut into cubes. Add water if necessary and boil until gravy is well thickened.

MRS. CLARA BITTNER.

Gumbo.

Cut into small pieces 6 tomatoes; 6 to 8 okras; 1 onion; 2 chili peppers; a little cabbage.

Add butter size of an egg, salt and pepper, a little water. Stew until tender.

MRS. H. W. BRAEUTIGAM.

Southern Gumbo.

Fry in cubes of bacon two tablespoons of rice until well browned, add small onion, sliced. Add to this 1 qt. sliced tomatoes; 1 qt. okra; 1 pod green pepper.

Cook one hour.

MRS. F. J. MAIER.

Kohl-Rabi a la Creme.

Peel and quarter and then cut them in thin slices and boil in slightly salted water.

Dissolve an ounce of butter, add to it a little flour, salt, nutmeg and white pepper to taste. Beat the yolk of one egg, add to it half a pint of milk, and beat it into the butter. When thick add the vegetable and serve. The leaves when tender are boiled and served as spinach.

MRS. B. L. ENDERLE.

Fried Okra.

Boil okra in salt water, adding 2 teaspoonfuls vinegar, cut lengthwise, dust with pepper and salt, dredge in cornmeal and fry in hot lard or butter until delicately browned.

MRS. LOUIS OEHLER.

Baked Potatoes and Herring.

3 ℔ potatoes; 2 or 3 salt herrings; 3 yolks and one egg; ¼ quart sour cream.

Parboil potatoes, slice. Let herrings soak in milk two or three hours to remove excessive salt. Bone carefully and chop. Place alternately in a baking dish, layers of potatoes and herring. Beat cream and eggs well, pour over potatoes and herring and bake in a moderate oven 1 to 1½ hours.

MRS. JOHN MAERZ.

Stuffed Tomatoes.

Select large tomatoes of even size, scoop out a small place and fill with either of the following dressings.

DRESSING No. 1.: Fry a small finely chopped onion in a tablespoonful of butter; when nearly done add some bread crumbs moistened with a little milk or water; season with salt and pepper. Put a little butter on each and bake.

DRESSING No. 2: Chop very fine cold meat or fowl of any kind with a very small piece of bacon; fry a finely chopped onion in a little butter, when nearly done add the meat, some bread crumbs, pepper and salt; cook a minute, add the yolk of 1 egg and fill the tomatoes; place them in a baking dish, sprinkle with bread crumbs add small bits of butter.

May be used as a garnish or served by itself.

MISS META DIETZ.

Spinach with Cheese Sauce.

Wash the spinach thoroughly and put in kettle of boiling water.

Add a tablespoon of salt and cook fifteen minutes without a cover.

SAUCE

2 tablespoons shortening; 2 tablespoons flour; 1 cup milk; ½ teaspoon salt; few grains pepper.

Melt the shortening and blend the flour, salt and pepper with it. Let thicken in double-boiler with the milk, then add the cup of grated cheese and stir until melted.

MRS. WM. MARSCHALL.

Spinach.

Soak 1 peck of spinach in cold water 1 hour; cover with boiling water, let boil until tender, about 30 minutes, take up and press all the water out of it. Place 2/3 cup of butter in sauce-pan, let boil up and mix 1 tablespoonful of flour to a smooth paste in it; put in spinach, let cook until butter is taken up, season with salt and black pepper to taste, put in ½ cup sweet cream, let it boil up once, and serve garnished with hard-boiled eggs.

MRS. W. C. CARTER.

Spinach.

Wash the spinach 3 or 4 times, pick carefully, and boil until tender. Drain well, and chop fine. Now put about 2 tablespoonfuls of finely chopped bacon into a saucepan, add a heaping tablespoon of slightly browned flour, and a small onion chopped fine. Add the spinach and about one cupful of soup stock, and salt and pepper to taste. Let boil up, and serve. Garnish with hard boiled eggs.

MRS. R. G. STRIEGLER.

Candied Sweet Potatoes.

Melt 1 cup sugar with ½ cup butter. Boil medium-sized potatoes, when nearly done, peel, slice and place in layers in a shallow pan, putting a tablespoon of the melted butter on each slice. Add 4 tablespoons hot water and bake ¾ hour, basting often.

MRS. F. J. MAIER.

Marshmallow Potatoes.

5 medium-sized potatoes, boiled in jackets. When done peel and mash, then add the following ingredients: 1 cupful milk, sugar and salt to taste, and 1 teaspoonful baking powder. Put butter size of an egg on top and bake in a baking dish. When done, cover with marshmallows, return to oven to brown, then serve hot.

MRS. FRITZ LUCKENBACH, Menard.

Spanish Tomatoes.

6 good sized tomatoes; 2 or 3 large sweet peppers; 2 onions; ½ cup milk; 1 tablespoon flour; 1 tablespoonful butter.

Cut peppers and onions in small pieces and cook in enough salt water to cover them.

When done add tomatoes which have been cooked in another vessel; let all cook together for a few minutes, put in a pinch of soda, let mixture boil up well, then add milk and flour beaten to a smooth paste. Just before removing from stove, put in salt and butter, serve very hot.

MRS. TEMPLE D. SMITH.

Stuffed Baked Tomatoes.

12 tomatoes; 1 small cabbage head; 1 medium sized onion; 1 cupful of sweet cream; bread crumbs, butter, pepper, sugar and salt.

From the blossom end of smooth, ripe and solid tomatoes, cut a thin slice; scoop out the pulp without breaking the rind surrounding it. Chop cabbage and onions fine, mix with fine bread crumbs and tomato pulp; season with pepper, salt and a little sugar; add the cream and mix well. Stuff the tomatoes; replace the slices, and place tomatoes (with cut ends up) in a baking dish with enough water to keep from burning. Drop a small lump of butter on each tomato and bake until tender. Place another small lump of butter on each tomato and serve in same dish. Very fine.

MISS BERTHA OCHS.

Baked Tomatoes.

Remove the skin from tomatoes and cut in halves. Roll in cracker crumbs that have been seasoned with salt and pepper, sprinkle tops with grated cheese and put in pan that has been greased. Bake 20 minutes.

MRS. WILLIE MARSCHALL.

Deviled Radishes.

Pare radishes and boil until tender, adding 1 teaspoonful of salt to water when nearly done. Place in a buttered, shallow glass baking-dish and sprinkle over 2 cupfuls of radishes, 1 tablespoonful of chopped nut meats, using walnuts or peanuts and 1 tablespoonful of grated cheese. Cover with rather thick and highly seasoned tomato sauce, sprinkle crumbs over thickly, grate 1 tablespoonful of cheese over all. Brown in a hot oven.

MRS. ALFRED P. C. PETSCH.

SALADS

Apple Salad.

Peel and dice about half a dozen apples. Beat 2 egg yolks, ½ teaspoon of lemon juice, salt, white pepper, 1 teaspoonful of mustard, 1 tablespoonful of vinegar, 1 tablespoonful of sugar and heat over slow fire until it begins to boil, stirring constantly. Then add 1 cup of cream, beat until it is cool. Pour over apples and mix thoroughly.

MRS. ARNOLD KOTT.

Beet Salad.

Cold boiled potatoes, beets, celery, in equal parts; 3 hard boiled eggs; 3 tablespoonfuls olive oil. Season to taste.

Dice the potatoes, beets, and celery. Mash the yolks of the eggs, add olive oil, salt and pepper and mix with the vegetables. Serve on lettuce leaves and garnish with rings of the hard boiled whites.

MRS. AUG. ITZ.

Celery Salad.

2 bunches celery; 1 tablespoon olive oil; 4 tablespoonfuls vinegar; sugar, pepper and salt to taste.

Wash and scrape celery; lay in ice-cold water until ready for use. Cut into inch lengths, mix with dressing and serve cold.

MRS. ED. OEHLER.

Cabbage Salad.

Medium sized head of cabbage; 1 large onion; 6 green sweet peppers; 6 medium sized tomatoes.

DRESSING: 1½ cup water, ½ cup vinegar; ½ cup sugar, 1 tablespoonful black pepper; 2 tablespoonfuls salt; ½ cup sweet cream.

MRS. AIB. KOENNECKE.

Cabbage Salad.

2 cups each of finely chopped cabbage and mellow apples, cover with boiled dressing made from the yolks of 2 eggs; 1 gill of vinegar; 2 gills milk; 1 tablespoon of butter; 1 teaspoonful of salt; 1 teaspoonful of mustard; ¼ teaspoonful of black pepper; carefully mixed and cooked in double-boiler. The cabbage should be soaked in cold water 1 hour before chopping and the dressing should be cold. Mix cabbage, apples and salad dressing and just before serving add 2 cups of finely chopped, roasted peanuts.

MRS. W. C. CARTER.

Cabbage Salad.

Medium sized head of cabbage; 1 large apple, chop up fine and salt; ½ cup chopped nuts.

Pour over this a dressing made of 2 eggs; 1 teaspoon butter; ½ cup pine-apple juice; a pinch of mustard and celery salt, and ½ cup vinegar.

This salad may be improved by adding 2 or 3 slices of pineapple.

MRS. OTTO KOLMEIER.

Mixed Salad.

6 large boiled potatoes (cold), diced; 3 barely ripe tomatoes; 1 onion, chopped; 3 hard-boiled eggs; 1 cucumber, sliced.

Season with salt, pepper and celery seed. Moisten with oil and vinegar or sour cream dressing. Must not be dry.

MRS. ROEHM.

Chicken Salad.

1 boiled chicken; 1 cup pecans; a few apples; a few pickles; some celery; six eggs; 1 tablespoonful sugar; 2 tablespoonfuls butter; ½ tablespoonful mustard; 1 cup cider vinegar; pepper and salt.

Chop the chicken, add pecans, apples, pickles and celery. Boil eggs hard. Rub the yolks of three eggs fine, add sugar, butter, mustard, vinegar, salt and pepper to taste. Mix all ingredients, put into a dish and decorate with three eggs cut into rings or lengthwise.

MRS. AUG. GOLD.

Chicken Salad.

1 boiled chicken; 2 small pickles; 1 cup pecans; 1 stalk celery; 2 apples; 6 eggs.

Chop chicken, pecans, apples, pickles and celery very fine. Boil eggs hard and cut in small squares, use half for salad and half to decorate the top of salad.

DRESSING: ½ teaspoon sugar; 2 eggs; ½ teaspoon mustard; ½ cup vinegar; ½ teaspoon salt; ½ cup water; ¼ teaspoon cayenne; 1 level tablespoon flour; 1 tablespoon butter.

Mix sugar, mustard, salt, cayenne and flour and beat well with the eggs, then add vinegar, water and butter, stir thoroughly, and then put in double boiler and let boil till it thickens. When cold mix with salad and serve.
MISS ANNA GOLD.

Chicken Salad.

Take 1 nice large hen, boil tender in salt water, then take from fire but let chicken remain in stock until cold. Cut up in 1/2 inch pieces, then take 1/2 the amount of blanched tender celery and also cut up in 1/3 inch pieces, and about 1 dozen olives cut in small pieces. When ready to serve mix with plenty of mayonnaise dressing.
MISS MARY STEIN.

Chicken Salad.

Put one good sized chicken on to cook in cold water, add one onion, simmer until chicken is very tender. Eight hard boiled egggs, one stalk celery or celery seed, six small dill pickles. Cut chicken, celery and pickles in small cubes. Chop the whites of eggs very fine, mixing all thoroughly. Then make a sauce of one cup butter, one-half cup olive oil, one-half cup vinegar, one large spoon mustard. Salt, pepper and sugar to taste.

Rub the yolks of eggs to a fine powder, then add the salt, pepper and sugar, then the oil and butter (which has been melted) putting in a few drops at a time, add mustard, lastly the vinegar, a spoonful at the time. Mix all ingredients well until the bottom of the mass is well saturated.

Mayonnaise dressing may be added if desired.
MRS. KURT KEIDEL.

Celery and Apple Salad.

1 bunch celery; 4 apples; dice very fine.

Season with salt and white pepper, and dress with a mixture of vinegar (1 tablespoonful) and double the amount thick cream. A tablespoon sugar may be added if preferred.

MRS. OTTO EVERS.

Italian Salad.

Any kind of meat cut into small squares, add same quantity of boiled potatoes cut into dice, 2 hard boiled eggs, 1 grated onion, 1 teaspoon of prepared mustard, 2 tablespoonfuls of cut pickles, 1 tablespoon cream, a little red pepper and salt. Mix with necessary vinegar and olive oil.

MRS. I. GLATZLE.

Salad of Celery Stalks.

1 head of cabbage; 12 celery stalks, chopped fine.

DRESSING: 1 cup vinegar; 1 tablespoon butter; 2 yolks of eggs (well beaten); 1 teaspoon salt; 1 teaspoon mustard; a pinch cayenne; 1 tablespoon sugar. Boil until thick. Beat dressing well and pour over salad.

MRS. ROEHM.

Marshmallow Salad.

2 cups marshmallows; 2 cups pineapples; 2 cups pecans.

Sweeten to taste; add whipped cream and a touch of mayonnaise dressing.

MRS. HENRY HIRSCH.

Fruit Salad.

1 cup seeded raisins or dates, 1 cup diced apples, 1 sliced banana, 1 shredded orange.

Mix with slightly sweetened and flavored whipped cream or mayonnaise. Sprinkle with chopped nuts and serve on lettuce leaves.   MISS AMANDA GROTE.

Fruit Salad.

1 cup nuts; 4 ripe apples; 4 bananas; ½ cup celery; ½ tablespoon melted butter; ½ tablespoon flour; ½ pint sweet milk; 1 egg; ¼ cup sugar; ½ cup vinegar; ¼ teaspoon mustard.

Chop fine the nuts, apples, bananas and celery and mix with the following dressing: Thicken the milk with the flour and butter rubbed to a smooth paste. Mix the beaten egg, sugar, vinegar, and mustard and add to the thickened milk stirring constantly until smooth.

MRS. AUG. JORDAN.

Fruit Salad.

Small box of pineapples; 3 apples; 3 bananas; 3 oranges; ¾ cup of pecans and dressing as follows:

Mix 4 tablespoons of sugar, 2 eggs, 2 tablespoonfuls of butter, the juice of the pineapples and 3 tablespoonfuls of vinegar. — Add vinegar last. Stir well, and cook until it thickens, stirring constantly. When cool add whipped cream.

MRS. R. G. STRIEGLER,
MRS. ROEHM.

Ham Salad.

2 ℔ boiled ham, cut in cubes; 3 chopped apples; ½ cup nuts; ½ cup vinegar; ½ cup celery, cut in small pieces. Salt and pepper to suit taste.

Mix well and before serving add the following dressing:

Yolks of 3 boiled eggs, rubbed to a paste; yolks of 2 raw eggs, well beaten. Mix thoroughly, add 1 tablespoon of vinegar, then add enough salad oil or melted butter to make it the consistency of cream.

MRS. MARY SCHWARZ.

Nut Salad.

4 apples; 2 cups celery; 2 cups nuts.

Peel and cut the apples; cut the celery and pecans and mix with the apples.

DRESSING: 1 cup vinegar; 1 tablespoon sugar; 1 tablespoon butter; yolks of 2 eggs; ½ cup water.

Cook vinegar and water, add butter, sugar, a pinch of salt, and pepper to taste. Beat eggs well and stir in quickly. Remove from fire and pour while hot over salad. Serve cold.

MRS. HERMAN USENER.

Nut Salad.

6 apples, cut in small slices; 2 bunches of celery, cut fine; 1 cup nuts; 2 tablespoonfuls whipped cream; 2 tablespoonfuls salad dressing.

MRS. LOUIS STIELER.

Herring Salad.

Soak 6 herring over night, remove skin and bones. 1 pound pork (may be omitted) cooked tender, 6 large irish potatoes boiled in jackets, 1 bunch celery, 5 large apples, 4 good sized sour pickles, 6 large canned or fresh beets, 5 hard boiled eggs. Cut all ingredients in small dice. Mix potatoes and beets first then add other ingredients. Then mix with a good mayonnaise dressing.

ELLA EVERS.

Potato Salad with Herring.

6 medium sized potatoes, boiled in their jackets; 3 hard boiled eggs; salt and pepper and onion to taste; 2 or 3 salt herrings, soaked at least 12 hours.

Slice potatoes, remove bones from herrings and cut into cubes; mix together.

Let come to a boil ½ cup vinegar, a tablespoonful of lard, salt, pepper, chopped onion and ½ cup water, pour over salad and serve cold.

MRS. FRITZ SIMON.

Picnic Salad.

½ qt. finely chopped cabbage; 6 apples; 1 cup nuts; 1 cup celery or 1 tablespoonful celery seed; 3 hard boiled eggs; 1 cup of cream. ..

DRESSING: 2 raw eggs, well beaten; 1 tablespoonful of mixed mustard; 1 tablespoonful of sugar; 4 tablespoonfuls of vinegar; salt to taste; a little white pepper.

Mix well, add the cream and pour over the mixture.

MRS. ROBERT BLUM.

Tomato Salad.

Peel and cut a slice from stem end of each tomato and remove the inside pulp. Pare 2 small cucumbers, cut in quarters and put in ice water until ready to mix, then dry and cut in thin slices. Mix with drained tomato pulp and moisten with mayonnaise. Arrange lettuce leaves, put in tomatoes filled with cucumber mixture and put 1 teaspoon mayonnaise on top of each.

MRS. CHAS. SCHWARZ.

Tomato Salad.

Remove stems of tomatoes, cut almost into halves, then into quarters and then into eighths, salt. Set in head of lettuce. One tablespoon diced pineapple, one tablespoon mayonnaise, add nuts if desired.

VERDIE KETTNER.

Surprise Salad.

Peel medium sized tomatoes, scoop out the pulp; chop cabbage and celery very fine, add a few broken walnut meats and mix with mayonnaise dressing; add a pinch of salt and pepper. Fill the tomatoes with the mixture and serve cold.

MRS. EDNA ALSTON.

Pear Salad.

Serve two halves of canned pears on lettuce leaves, grate cheese over the pears, and put mayonnaise on top.

MRS. P. W. LEMONS.

Harvard Salad.

Cover large green pepper with ice water and let stand until crisp. Cut a slice from stem, remove seeds, and wipe out inside.

Mash cream cheese, moisten with cream and season with salt and cayenne pepper. Fill pepper case with cheese, chill thoroughly, and cut in 1/3 inch slices crosswise. Drain slices of canned pineapple, and serve a slice of pepper and cheese on top of a slice of pineapple on lettuce leaves with a teaspoon of mayonnaise on top.

MRS. P. W. LEMONS.

Salmon Salad.

1 can salmon; 2 sweet peppers; 2 cabbage leaves; 4 pickles; 1 large apple; 2 hard boiled eggs; ½ teaspoon salt; ¼ teaspoon black pepper; 1 tablespoonful butter melted; ½ cup vinegar.

Slice cabbage, sweet peppers, pickles and apples very fine, dice hard boiled eggs, add salt, pepper, butter and vinegar; pour over salmon and mix well.

MRS. D. A. RILEY.

Fruit Salad Dressing.

½ cup sugar; ½ teaspoon mustard; ½ teaspoon salt; ¼ teaspoon cayenne; 4 tablespoonfuls butter; 4 tablespoonfuls vinegar; 1 cup whipped cream; 3 yolks of eggs.

Mix seasoning with butter melted, add eggs and vinegar, boil in a pan of water until thick; when cold, add cup of cream.

MISS ANNA GOLD.

Fruit Salad.

1 grape fruit; 3 oranges; 3 slices pineapple; 12 marshmallows; ¼ cup of chopped nut meats; 1 apple.

MISS OLGA VON HAGEN.

Salad.

1 can salmon; 4 sour pickles, chopped fine; 2 hard boiled eggs; 1 level teaspoon mustard; 1 tablespoon sugar; 1 tablespoon butter; 2 tablespoons cream or milk; 6 tablespoons vinegar; 1 raw egg.

MRS. A. W. MOURSUND.

Tomato Aspic Salad.

Dissolve 2 tablespoonfuls of gelatine in ½ cupful of cold water. Turn the contents of a can of tomatoes or ½ dozen fresh tomatoes into a porcelain lined saucepan; add 1 teaspoonful of cloves and allspice, 2 tablespoonfuls of sugar, ½ teaspoonful of black pepper, add salt to taste. Cook about 20 minutes, strain, and again put on the fire to boil. Mix with the soaked gelatine. Turn into molds and set on ice.

MRS. FELIX KLAERNER.

Vegetable Salad.

6 potatoes; 3 tablespoonfuls pickles; 2 apples; 1 green pepper; ½ head cabbage; 2 onions; 3 egg yolks; butter size of an egg.

DRESSING: 1 teaspoonful celery seed; a pinch of pepper; ½ cupful vinegar; ½ teaspoonful Worcestershire Sauce; 1 teaspoonful salt; ¼ cupful sugar; 1 tablespoonful butter; 2 egg yolks.

Boil the potatoes, slice thin, chop cabbage, pickles, onions and apples. Boil eggs hard, chop fine, cut pepper fine, and mix all ingredients. Heat butter and vinegar; add other ingredients, let them come to a boil; add beaten yolks of eggs, stir until it thickens and remove from fire. Cool, and when the salad is ready to serve, mix with the dressing.

MRS. AUG. GOLD.

Combination Vegetable Salad.

Marinate in French dressing two cupfuls each of cold cooked asparagus tips and tiny whole new cooked potatoes. Drain and arrange in layers in a Salad bowl which has been rubbed with a split clove of garlic. Between each layer add a few slices of cooked young turnips, cooked young carrots, peeled and sliced radishes, diced celery, and sliced spring onions. Serve with the following Chiffonade dressing:

Mix 2 tablespoonfuls of vinegar with 5 tablespoonfuls of olive oil and half a teaspoonful each of salt and paprika, beat together, and add 1 cooked beet, 1 hard cooked egg and a few pecans, all chopped fine.

MRS. VIDA G. NEWBERRY.

Fruit Salad Dressing.

2 eggs; 3 tablespoonfuls of melted butter; 3 tablespoonfuls of lemon juice; ½ teaspoonful of salt; 1 cup of sweet cream; ¼ cup of powdered sugar; ½ teaspoonful of vanilla.

Beat the sugar, egg, butter and lemon juice together until very light. Cook over hot water until mixture thickens. Cool, then add salt, vanilla and cream which has been whipped till stiff.

Serve cold on any fruit salad.

MRS. EMIL RILEY.

Salad Dressing.

2 eggs, yolks beaten separately; 1 tablespoon sugar; 1 teaspoon salt; 4 tablespoons vinegar. Cook this until thick, stirring it all the time. Remove from fire and stir in the beaten whites. When ready to use stir in 1 cup whipped cream if desired.

MRS. L. K. TAINTER.

Salad Dressing.

4 tablespoonfuls of butter; 1 tablespoonful of flour; 1 cup sweet milk; 2 eggs; 1 teaspoonful of mustard; 2 tablespoonfuls of sugar; 1 teaspoonful of salt; ½ cup of vinegar.

Mix flour and butter, when melted, add sweet milk, let come to a boil. Mix mustard, sugar, salt, vinegar, and eggs; add the milk and let boil until thick. Remove from fire and beat well for a few minutes.

MRS. E. VANDER STUCKEN.

Mayonnaise Dressing (Without Oil.)

2 eggs; butter, size of an egg; 1 tablespoon mixed mustard; 1 teaspoon salt; 3 tablespoonfuls of vinegar; 1 tablespoonful sugar.

Beat eggs, add mustard, salt and sugar, beat again and add melted butter and vinegar. Set bowl over boiling water and stir constantly until thick and smooth. When cold, add a cupful of whipped cream.

MRS. H. W. KUSENBERGER.

Mayonnaise Dressing.

Have dishes and ingredients very cold. In summer set dish in pan of crushed ice. In soup-plate or shallow bowl put yolk of 1 raw egg, add ¼ teaspoonful salt and a dash cayenne, stir with fork till very thick. Add a few drops of olive oil and stirr; add more oil, few drops at a time until mixture balls on fork. Thin with few drops lemon juice, then add more oil. Alternate in this way until 1 cup of olive oil is used and dressing is thick and glossy like jelly. About 3 tablespoons lemon juice will be needed. Always stir in the same direction. Keep covered and on ice until needed.

MRS. J. A. SCHLEYER.

Mayonnaise Dressing for Pressed Chicken.

3 eggs well beaten; ½ cup of sugar; ½ teaspoon of black pepper; a pinch of cayenne pepper; ½ teaspoonful of mustard; 1 tablespoonful of olive oil; 1 tablespoonful of butter; 1 cup of vinegar.

Boil thick. MRS. LOUIS DIETZ.

Simple Salad Dressing.

Butter, size of walnut; 2 tablespoons of sugar; 1 teaspoon mustard; 1 teaspoon salt; 1 teaspoon cornstarch; 2 eggs; 1 teacup mild vinegar.

Mix butter, cornstarch, mustard and salt together; add beaten eggs and sugar; cook until thick in double boiling pan and add vinegar last. Thin with cream when wanted for use.

MRS. G. L. STEBBINS.

Mayonnaise Dressing.

Take the yolks of 2 eggs, beat with a fork, then take ½ cup of good fresh olive oil, add only 1 drop at a time, beat continually until all the oil is used, then add salt to taste, also a dash of cayenne pepper, and the juice of 1 lemon, then add 1 cupful of whipped cream and a little sugar, mustard may also be added.

All ingredients should be ice-cold before making.

This is a dressing for any salad. Cream should not be added until the dressing is used. Will keep a week on ice. If olives are added this dressing makes a splendid filling for sandwiches.

MISS MARY STEIN.

PUDDINGS

Apple Pudding.

Stew ½ doz. apples with ½ cup sugar and pour in pudding dish.

Make custard of 1 qt. milk, yolks of 3 eggs, ½ cup sugar, 3 tablespoonfuls flour; pour this over the apples.

Beat the whites of the eggs to a stiff froth, add a little sugar, pour on custard; place in oven for a few moments to brown.

MRS. H. W. BRAEUTIGAM.

Bread Pudding.

Soak 2 cups bread crumbs in 4 cups hot milk, then mash well with a wire potato masher. Beat 2 eggs with 2/3 cup sugar and ¼ teaspoon salt. Add the milk and bread to this; then flavor with 1 teaspoonful vanilla and 2 teaspoons of melted butter. Bake in a slow oven or cook in a steamer until firm (about ½ hour), serve hot with sauce.

E. LOUDON.

Cocoanut Custard.

1 cup cocoanut; ½ lb powdered sugar; 1 quart milk; 6 eggs beaten; 1 teaspoon nutmeg; 2 teaspoons vanilla.

Boil the milk, whip in gradually the beaten eggs. When nearly cold add cocoanut, pour in paste shells. Bake 20 minutes.

MRS. EMIL WEBER.

Frozen Banana Pudding.

Four bananas; 1 heaping teaspoon powdered gelatine; 4 tablespoonfuls sugar; 3 tablespoonfuls boiling water; 3 cups milk; 1 cup whipped cream; 3 eggs.

Put the gelatine in a sauce-pan, add the eggs, water, sugar and milk; stir until they thicken, then cool and add the bananas rubbed through a sieve and the whipped cream.

Freeze and serve with cherries on top.

MRS. JOHN KELLER.

Orange Pudding.

Peel and slice 4 large oranges, put in pudding pan and sprinkle with 1 cup of sugar.

Make a boiled custard of 1 quart milk; yolks of 3 eggs, well beaten; ½ cup sugar; 2 tablespoonfuls cornstarch. When cool pour over oranges. Over this spread the whites of the eggs beaten with four tablespoonfuls sugar, place in oven and brown.

MRS. H. CORDES.

Christmas Pudding.

½ lb stale bread crumbs; 1 cup scalded milk; 2/3 cup sugar; 5 eggs; 1½ cups raisins; 2/3 cup currants; ½ cup pecans or walnuts; ½ cup citron; ½ lb suet; ¼ cup brandy; ½ nutmeg; ¾ teaspoon cinnamon; ¾ teaspoon mace; 1½ teaspoon salt.

Soak the crumbs in the milk. Add the sugar, the well beaten eggs, the raisins (seeded, cut in pieces, and dredged in flour) currants, pecans, citron (cut in strips), and the chopped suet. When thoroughly blended add the brandy, salt, and spices. Turn into buttered mold and steam or boil six hours. Serve with foamy sauce.

Foamy Sauce.

½ cup butter; 1 cup powdered sugar; whites of 2 eggs; ½ cup rich whipped cream; salt.

Cream butter and sugar. Put over hot water, add beaten whites, and beat until well blended. Cool, add a little salt, and the whipped cream. Then beat again.

MRS. A. W. MOURSUND.

Date Jelly.

Take a package of good dates, remove the pits and fill with chopped walnuts or pecans; pour 1 to 2 pints strawberry gelatine into a mold and when it begins to harden, repeat the process using in all 1 pt. orange and 1 pt. strawberry gelatine. Place on ice until perfectly firm. Serve with whipped cream.

MRS. JOHN KELLER.

Maltese Rice.

1 cup large grained rice; 2 or 3 lemons, grated rind of one; ½ cup sugar or more according to taste; 2 cups water.

Make a rich lemonade, adding by way of flavoring a tablespoon of rum or brandy. Swell rice in 6 cups water in a double-boiler or oven; never use salt in the preparation of this dish.

Pour lemonade over rice allowing same to boil up once in the mixture, pour in mold and set to cool. May be improved by adding chopped almonds. Orange juice or pineapple in addition to the lemon makes a rich and delicious dessert.

MRS. H. GOLDSCHMIDT.

Marshmallow Pudding.

Whites of 4 eggs, beaten right stiff; add ¾ cup of sugar. Dissolve 1 tablespoon of Knox gelatine in ¼ cup of cold water, add ¼ cup boiling water, add this a little at the time to the eggs, while beating, flavor to suit taste. To half of froth add a little fruit coloring and sprinkle with pecans or any fruit. Put the white froth on top. Set on ice to harden. Serve with cream.

MRS. HILMAR WEBER
MISS BERTHA OCHS.

Apple Roll.

2 cups flour, 4 level teaspoons baking powder; ½ teaspoon salt, 3 level tablespoons shortening; ½ cupful liquid, half water and half milk; 4 apples chopped fine. Roll dough ½ inch thick spread with apples. Roll then cut 1½ or 2 inches long, place cut side down in hot syrup, made by boiling 1 pint water and 1½ cups sugar. Put a piece of butter on top of each, sprinkle with sugar and nutmeg. Then bake; serve with cream.

MRS. L. K. TAINTER.

Peach Pudding.

Put 4 cupfuls of peaches in a pudding dish, set on stove to heat. Make batter of 2 eggs, 2 cupfuls sweet milk; 2 tablespoonfuls of butter; 2½ cups of flour; 1 teaspoonful of baking powder and a pinch of salt. When fruit is boiling hot, pour batter over it, and bake until thoroughly done. Serve with sugar and cream.

MRS. MAX SCHOENEWOLF.

Peach Dumplings.

2 cups flour; 4 teaspoons baking powder; 2 tablespoons Crisco; 1 teaspoon salt; ¾ cup milk.

6 peaches; ¼ cup sugar. Mix and sift all dry ingredients. Work in the Crisco and add milk to make a soft dough. Roll to ¼ inch thickness, and shape with biscuit cutter. Cut peaches in halves, extract its pit and put sugar in its place. Cover again with other half peach, and put between 2 biscuits and press edges together. Bake 30 minutes. Serve with cream.

MRS. MAX SCHOENEWOLF.

Lemon Cream.

3 tablespoonfuls cornstarch; juice and rind of 1½ lemons; 1 cupful sugar; 2 eggs; ½ teaspoonful salt; 2½ cupfuls boiling water.

Mix cornstarch with one-half of the sugar; add the boiling water gradually and cook 15 minutes in a double boiler. Add the egg yolks beaten with the rest of the sugar, the salt, and lemon juice; cook 5 minutes longer. Pour this mixture into the stiffly beaten egg whites, whip vigorously, chill, and serve piled high in sherbet glasses.

ELLA WAHRMUND.

Lemon Foam Pudding.

Put 2 cups of hot water; 1 cup granulated sugar into saucepan. When it boils add 2 rounded tablespoons of cornstarch dissolved in a little cold water. Stir fast as it boils. After it has cooked 4 or 5 minutes squeeze in the juice of a lemon. Take from stove and let cool. Whip to a stiff froth the whites of 2 eggs—3 when eggs are cheap. By this time the cooked cornstarch which has been stirred occasionally is cool enough to be poured slowly over the whites of eggs, a brisk whipping going on meantime. In about one minute the whole mass will be light and foamy. Set in cool place. A custard made of 1 pint of milk and the beaten yolks of the eggs may be poured over the "Lemon Foam" when it is served, though it is not essential.

MRS. WM. MARSCHALL.

Nut and Tapioca Pudding.

1½ cupfuls of tapioca; 2½ cupfuls of sugar; 1 cup chopped nut meats; 1 can pineapple; strained juice of 1 lemon; strained juice of 1 orange; whites of 2 eggs; whipped cream.

Cover tapioca with cold water and allow it to soak over night. Put it into a saucepan with the sugar and allow to cook until clear then add nut meats, orange and lemon juice and the syrup from the can of pineapple; fold in the stiffly beaten whites of eggs. Serve cold with whipped cream.

MRS. MAX WINKEL.

Fruit Crown. (Dessert.)

Heat 2 pints of water and prepare with 2 packages of Raspberry or Strawberry Jello. Then prepare separately 1 pint of Lemon Jello, or 1 pint of Pineapple juice, to which one package of gelatine has been added. Cover bottom of wet mold with a little Raspberry juice (about 1/3 of whole proportion). When set, pour in lemon or pineapple jelly, whipped to a sponge, mixed with half a cup of cherries or nuts. When set, add the remainder of Raspberry jelly.

MRS. GEO. E. KOTT.

Baked Custard.

Beat 5 eggs; 5 tablespoons sugar; 1 qt. milk; ½ teaspoon vanilla. Bake in a moderate oven until firm. If desired pour the custard into cups, set in a pan of water, and bake twenty minutes. Serve with vanilla or any other sauce. MRS. VICTOR KEIDEL.

Pineapple Tapioca Pudding.

3 cups boiling water; ¾ cups Minute Tapioca; boil ten minutes.

Add small can grated pineapple, and 1 cup sugar. Cook 3 minutes then stir in whites of 3 eggs. When cool, set in ice box till stiff. Serve with cream, plain or whipped. MRS. ELISE REINBACH.

Rice Pudding.

½ cup rice; 1½ pint milk; ½ cup sugar; a little salt; 1 tablespoon lemon rind or flavor.

Put washed rice, sugar, salt and milk in pudding dish, bake in moderate oven 2 hours, stirring frequently first 1½ hours, then permit it to finish cooking with a light colored crust, disturbing it no more. Eat cold with cream or any sauce.

MRS. ELISE REINBACH.

Bishop Whipple Pudding.

1 cup chopped pecans; 1 cup chopped dates; ½ cup sugar; 2/3 cups flour; 2 eggs; 1 teaspoon baking powder.

Mix as cake, except that you beat whites and yolks of eggs together. Bake in biscuit pan. Break in pieces while hot, and sprinkle with powdered sugar. Serve cold with whipped cream.

MRS. O. B. WITTE.

Cabinet Pudding.

6 eggs; 6 tablespoons sugar; 10 cocoanut macaroons; 1 pint of cherries; 2 tablespoons Knox gelatine; 1 cup of pecan meats; 1/3 cup of sweet milk; ¼ cup of wine. Take the yolks of eggs, the milk, sugar and juice from cherries and make a custard in double boiler. Soak gelatine in a cup of water and add to custard. Then add the stiffly beaten whites of the eggs, the crumbled macaroons, chopped nut meats and the cherries, cut fine. Mix all well and set aside to harden. Chill and serve with whipped cream.

MRS. P. W. LEMONS.

Apple Snow.

1 qt. of milk; 6 eggs; 6 apples; 4 tablespoons sugar; ½ teaspoon vanilla. Let milk come to a boil. Beat sugar and yolks of eggs well, then stir same into the milk. Continue stirring to prevent curdling. Add a pinch of salt. Set aside to cool, then add vanilla flavoring. Before serving beat the whites of the eggs to a stiff froth, with ½ cup of sugar. Grate and add apples. Drop by spoonfuls on custard.

MRS. VICTOR KEIDEL.

Caramel Pudding.

6 tablespoons white sugar, browned to syrup in iron saucepan. 3 eggs beaten together, ½ cup of milk; 3 tablespoons sugar; 1 teaspoon vanilla. Beat together; pour syrup into six cups and the mixture over it. Set in pan of hot water; cook twenty minutes.

MRS. O. B. WITTE.

Pastry, Pies, Tarts

Pie Crust.

1 cupful flour; 5 tablespoonfuls lard or butter; ½ teaspoonful salt; about 2 tablespoonfuls water.

Sift flour, mix in lard, then cold water; place dough on board and roll out from center, using a light motion. This will make two crusts.

MISS MARY STEIN.

Pie Crust.

¾ cup of lard; ½ cup of water; 2 cups of flour; ½ teaspoonful of salt.

Always in adding the filler in a pie, let the crust be thoroughly cool.

MRS. E. VANDER STUCKEN.

Schaum-Torte. (Pastry.)

1 cup cream; flour sufficient to handle; ¼ cup water; pinch salt (mix well).

Roll out ½ inch thick in platter spread with butter, fold over and roll out again. Repeat this once more. Bake in deep dish.

When cold spread jelly over and cover with whipped cream.

In place of whipped cream an extra sweet meringue may be used.

MRS. FRITZ KNUST.

Banana Pie.

1 qt. sweet milk; 4 eggs; ¾ cup sugar; 1 teaspoonful cornstarch.

Cook the milk, sugar, cornstarch and yolks of eggs till thick; after crust is baked fill with sliced bananas; pour the custard over this. Beat the whites with 6 tablespoonfuls sugar, spread on top of pie, and bake to a nice brown.

MRS. H. CORDES.

Apple Pie.

½ cup cream; 1 egg; 6 boiled apples; 1 teaspoon vanilla; butter size of a walnut; sugar to taste.

Beat sugar, cream, flavoring, and egg.

Place apples on crust, pour liquid over, dab with bits of butter, and bake in moderate oven.

MRS. I. GLATZLE.

Banana Pie.

FILLING: 1 pint of sweet milk; ½ cup of sugar; 1 teaspoonful of vanilla; 2 yolks of eggs; 2 tablespoons of flour.

Cook together in double boiler until thick.

PIE CRUST: 1 cupful of flour; 2 tablespoons ice water; 4 level tablespoonfuls lard.

Bake crust. Cover with layer of sliced bananas and put in the filling. Beat the whites of the two eggs, adding two tablespoons of sugar. Place on top and brown in the oven.

MARY LOVE.

Apple Cream Pie.

To 2 cups of stewed and mashed apples add ¾ cup sugar, put on crust and bake. When cold pour over it 1 cup of sweet cream whipped with 3 tablespoonfuls sugar.

MRS. H. CORDES.

Buttermilk Pie.

1 cup buttermilk; 2 eggs; ¾ cup sugar; 1 teaspoon cornstarch; juice and rind of ½ lemon.

Mix, pour in crust and bake. When done spread with eggwhites beaten with 3 tablespoons sugar; set in oven to brown.

MRS. H. CORDES.

Chocolate Pie.

2 cups of milk; 1 cup of sugar; yolks of 3 eggs; 3 tablespoonfuls of flour; 3 tablespoonfuls of cocoa; 1 teaspoonful of vanilla.

Boil until thick and smooth. Bake crust and fill. Beat whites of eggs, add 3 tablespoonfuls of sugar. Brown.

MRS. ROEHM.

Cream Pie.

½ cup sugar; 1 tablespoon butter; 2 tablespoons flour; 2 well beaten eggs; 2 cups rich milk; 2 teaspoons orange extract.

MRS. MOURSUND.

Blackberry Short Cake.

1 qt. of flour; 1 teaspoonful of salt; 2 heaping teaspoonfuls baking powder; 2 tablespoonfuls butter: pint of milk.

Sift the flour, salt and baking powder together.

mix in the butter cold, add the milk and mix into a smooth dough, just soft enough to handle. Divide in two, roll out one-half inch thick to size of pie plate. Brush first layer with melted butter and lay on greased pie plate. Bake in hot oven twenty minutes, separate the cakes without cutting.

Put one quart of blackberries in earthen bowl, sprinkle with sugar, crush slightly and spread on cut side of hot short cake. Put on the other cake. Spread top with whipped cream sweetened with a little sugar and flavored with vanilla. Garnish the top with whole blackberries.

MRS. OTTO DITTMAR.

Cream Cheese Pie.

1 soup plate cream cheese; ½ cup sugar; 1 cup currants; 3 eggs; 1 teaspoon vanilla.

Smooth cheese with mixing spoon, adding cream or milk if too dry. Stir in sugar, currants, flavoring, the yolks of eggs and the beaten white of one egg. Fill into pie crust and bake. Reserve remaining whites of egg for meringue.

If pie is preferred without meringue, sprinkle with sugar and cinnamon.

MRS. H. GOLDSCMIDT.

Lemon Pie.

2 small cups sugar; 6 level tablespoonfuls flour; 2 lemons; 1 orange; 6 eggs; 2 cups of water.

Line a pie pan with rich crust. Mix the flour with sugar, grate the rind of one lemon and half the rind of the orange, use juice of all three, mix well with sugar, add the yolks of eggs, stir well and add the water, fill the pie crust and bake till thick custard.

Beat the whites of eggs to a stiff froth, add one half cup sugar, beat stiff, spread on pie set in oven again, and bake till light brown.

This makes two pies.

MISS ANNA GOLD.

Cream Pie.

Yolks of 5 eggs; 1 teaspoon butter; 1 pt. sugar; 1 pint rich cream; 1 tablespoon flour.

Custard Pie.

Yolks of 5 eggs; 6 tablespoons sugar; 2 cups milk; 1 teaspoon butter; 2 tablespoons flour or cornstarch. Flavor to taste.

Cocoanut Pie.

1 pint milk; 3 eggs; ½ cup cocoanut; 1 teaspoon cornstarch; sugar to taste.

Bake in a rich pie crust.

MRS. A. KUENEMANN.

Jelly Pie.

1 tablespoonful of butter; 2 tablespoonfuls of sugar; 1 large egg; ½ cupful of jelly or jam.

Make a crust of biscuit dough, line pie tin and place in oven long enough to dry on top. Pour in the filling and bake (without an upper crust) in a hot oven to a dark brown.

MRS. F. STEIN.

Lemon Pie.

2 eggs; juice and rind of ½ lemon; 1 tablespoonful cornstarch; 6 tablespoonfuls water; 6 tablespoonfuls sugar.

Mix the yolks of the eggs with 3 tablespoonfuls of the sugar, lemon, starch, butter and water, pour over crust and bake.

Beat the whites of the 2 eggs with the rest of the sugar, spread on pie when done, put back in oven till a nice brown.

MRS. H. CORDES.

Lemon Pie.

1 cup water; 1 cup sugar; 2 tablespoonfuls flour; 4 eggs; juice of 1 lemon.

Boil together sugar, water, flour and lemon juice; when cold add yolks of eggs.

Line pie plates with rich paste fill with custard and bake.

Beat whites of eggs with a little sugar spread over pies and put back in oven long enough to brown nicely.

MRS. HY. BASSE.

Summer Mince Pie.

1 cup of crushed crackers; 1 cup of boiling water; 1 cup of molasses; 1 cup of sugar; ½ cup of vinegar; ½ cup of melted butter; 1 large cup of raisins; 1 teaspoonful of allspice; 1 teaspoonful of cinnamon; ½ teaspoon of cloves; ½ teaspoon of pepper; 1 small nutmeg.

Chop raisins, then add all ingredients, water and vinegar last. Bake between two crusts.

MRS. BERTHA NAUWALD.

Pecan Custard Pie.

2 cups of sugar; 1 cup of water; butter size of an egg; 4 eggs; 2 teaspoonfuls of cornstarch; 1 cup of cream or rich milk; 1½ cups finely chopped pecans; vanilla to suit taste.

Boil sugar and water to a thick syrup, to this add the butter. Take the yolks of the four eggs, add cornstarch and milk or cream. To this add the syrup, place on the stove and boil till it thickens. Add flavor and pecans. Pour into baked crust. Make icing of whites, spread on top, put in oven until browned.

MRS. WECK MEARS,
Menard, Texas.

Molasses Pie.

1 cup sugar; ½ cup butter; ½ cup molasses; ½ cup rich cream; yolks of 4 eggs.

Mix well and cook until a thick cream, fill baked crust. Spread with the whites of 2 eggs beaten to a stiff froth with ½ cup sugar, and brown lightly.

MRS. MOURSUND.

Sand Tarts.

2 eggs, reserving the whites of one; 2 cups sugar; 1 cup butter; 3 cups flour.

Mix in the usual manner, roll out thin, cut out with a doughnut-cutter, spread with the white of one egg, sprinkle with sugar and cinnamon, and place an almond or raisin in the center of each cake. Bake in a quick oven.

MISS BERTHA PRIESS.

Pumpkin Pie.

4 eggs; 1 quart of pumpkin, strained; 3 cups sugar; 1 teaspoonful of ginger; 3 pints milk; 4 teaspoonfuls of cinnamon.

Boil pumpkin, strain, add sugar, milk and yolks of eggs, and spices; beat together thoroughly and put in pie crust and bake.

Then have ready the whites of eggs beaten very stiff with ½ cup sugar, spread on top and set in oven to bake a light brown.

For pie crust use: 2 cups flour; 4 heaping teaspoonfuls lard, and a little salt.

Rub lard in flour well and add cold water enough to make a stiff dough. Roll out thin and line your piepans. This is enough for two pies.

MISS ALVINA GOLD.

Pumpkin or Squash Pie. No. 1.

3 cups stewed and strained pumpkins; 2 cups milk; 2 eggs; 1 cup sugar; ½ teaspoon cinnamon; 1 teaspoon salt; pinch cloves.

Line 2 pieplates with crust as for custard pie and bake in moderate oven.

MRS. ED. OEHLER.

Delicious Pumpkin Pie. No. 2.

3 eggs; 1 quart of strained pumpkin; 2 cupfuls sugar; 2 tablespoonfuls of butter; 1 teaspoonful of cinnamon. Orange extract to taste.

Put in pie crust and bake.

MRS. LEWIS K. SMITH.

Pecan Pie.

1 cup sweet milk; 1 cup sugar; 2 tablespoons flour; ½ cup chopped pecans; 3 eggs.

Mix sugar and flour, add milk, eggs well beaten and pecans.

PIE-CRUST: 3 cups flour; ½ teaspoon salt; 1 cup lard; ice-water.

Rub lard through flour; mix in the ice-water, add salt. Handle as little as possible, roll thin, lop over, and roll again. Fill crust and bake until nearly done, cover with meringue, set back in oven to brown, and sprinkle with chopped nuts.

MRS. ERWIN NEFFENDORF.

Orange Cream Pie.

1 teaspoon of cornstarch; ½ tablespoon of sugar; juice of one orange; rind of ¼ orange; ¾ cup of water; 1 tablespoon of Karo Syrup; juice of one lemon; yolks of two eggs.

Place in sauce-pan over the fire the cornstarch, water, sugar and Karo. Boil five minutes, remove from fire, add yolks of eggs, orange rind and juices of lemon and orange.

Line pie pan with very thin crust, brush with beaten white of egg, add pie mixture and bake in moderate oven.

MRS. HARRY M. HARRINGTON.

Orange Pie. No. 2.

1 cupful sugar; 3 tablespoonfuls flour; 3 oranges.

Slice oranges on crust, sprinkle with sugar and flour mixed, and bake.

MRS. HUGO BORGFELD.

Berry Muffins.

¼ cupful of butter; 1/3 cupful of sugar; 1 egg; 2 1/3 cupfuls of flour; 3 teaspoonfuls of baking powder; ½ teaspoonful of salt; 1 cupful of milk; 1 cupful of berries; 1/3 cupful of flour.

Cream butter, add gradually the sugar and well beaten egg. Mix flour, baking powder and salt. Add alternately with the milk to the first mixture; then add the berries rolled in one-third cupful of flour. Fill hot buttered gem pans two-thirds full. Bake twenty-five minutes.

MRS. OTTO DITTMAR.

Jeff Davis Pie.

3 eggs; 1 large cup sweet milk; ½ cup sugar; 3 tablespoonfuls flour; 1 tablespoon butter.

Beat yolks, add butter, sugar and flour. Then add milk and any desired flavoring, turn in flaky crust and bake. When done, have the 3 egg whites beaten stiff with 3 tablespoons sugar, to spread on top and brown.

MRS. ED. WINKEL.

Butter-Scotch Pie.

2 cups milk; 1 cup brown sugar; 2 tablespoons cornstarch, 3 tablespoons butter; ¼ teaspoon salt; 2 eggs; 1 teaspoon vanilla, pastry crust, marshmallows.

Scald milk in double boiler, mix sugar and cornstarch, add to milk, stir until thick, cover and cook 15 minutes. Add butter and salt and pour over egg yolks slightly beaten.

Return to double boiler, stir and cook one minute, remove from fire and cool. When ready to serve, add vanilla and pour into baked pastry crust.

Cut marshmallows in pieces and put in a warm place until they are soft. Beat egg whites until stiff, beat in marshmallows, and spread over the top of the pie. Serve as it is or if desired bake in the oven until delicately browned.

ELLA WAHRMUND.

Sweet Potato Pie.

1 pound steamed sweet potatoes finely mashed; 2 cups sugar; 1 cup cream; ½ cup butter; 3 beaten eggs. Flavor with lemon or nutmeg.

Beat well and pour into pie tins lined with good pie crust.

MRS. ED. STEIN.

Blaetter Squares.

3 eggs; 3 tablespoonfuls of water; 1 tablespoonful of vinegar. Add flour to stiffen, roll out thin, spread with butter, roll again and spread with butter. Keep this up until one pound of butter is used, then spread top with butter, sugar and cinnamon, cut into squares, and bake in a hot oven.

MRS. HENZE.

Peanut Butter Pie.

3 eggs; 4 tablespoons sugar; 2 tablespoons butter; 2 tablespoons peanut butter; ½ cup sweet milk.

Mix ingredients together; fill crust and bake a delicate brown.

Use whites of 3 eggs for meringue. These proportions make one pie.

MRS. O. B. WITTE.

BREAD, COFFEE CAKE, DOUGHNUTS, ETC.

Bread.

1 quart buttermilk; ½ cup sugar; 1 tablespoon salt; 1 small cup mashed potatoes; 1 yeast cake; flour; 1 pint warm water.

Scald the buttermilk and while hot, add the sugar, salt and potatoes. When cool add the yeast previously soaked in warm water. Let stand twelve or eighteen hours before using. Stir in flour to make a thin batter and let rise. If more bread is wanted when making up add some water and salt. Let rise once or twice. Be sure and work well.

MRS. A. W. MOURSUND.

Light Bread.

1 yeast cake to 3 loaves; 1 quart luke-warm water; 2 teaspoons salt, tablespoon sugar, 2 tablespoonfuls lard; 2 quarts flour.

Dissolve yeast cake in ½ qt. warm water, adding sugar and ½ sieve flour; beat well and let stand over night in a warm place to rise. Next morning add salt, about ½ qt. water, melted lard and enough flour to form stiff dough. Set aside again to rise, then form into loaves, let rise again and bake in moderate oven. Glaze with hot water or lard.

Brown Bread.

¾ cup No. 6 molasses; 2 cups graham flour; 1 cup sweet milk; 2 level teaspoons soda in syrup; pinch of salt; 1 cup seeded raisins.

Put in large baking powder can, set in bucket of water, cover and steam 3 hours.

MISS ADA PEDEN.

Nut Bread.

1 cup sugar; 1 cup nuts; ½ cup sweet milk; 1 egg; 4 teaspoons baking powder; 4 cups flour.

Stir and put in pan to rise, let stand 20 minutes. It will about double itself. Put in moderate oven and bake 1 hour.

MISS ADA PEDEN.

Buttermilk Yeast Cakes.

Dissolve 1 yeast cake in 1 pint of warm water, add 1 tablespoon each of cornmeal and sugar and 1 teaspoonful of salt. Let stand over night.

In the morning boil 1 pint of buttermilk, have ready 1 cup of flour and water, mixed to a smooth, stiff batter; pour this into the boiling milk and let it cook thoroughly, stirring constantly. When cool add to the yeast cake mixture which has stood over night and set in a warm place until it ferments. Then work in corn meal enough to make a tolerably stiff dough, mold into cakes and dry in the shade.

MRS. JACOB GOLD, SR.

Yeast Cakes.

3 large Irish potatoes; 1½ tablespoonfuls of hops; 2 tablespoonfuls of sugar; ½ tablespoonful of ginger; cornmeal; 1½ qts. of water; 1 cup of flour; 1 cup of dissolved yeast; small handful of salt.

Peel the potatoes and cook with the hops, (tied in a cloth) in about 1½ qts. of water. Mash the potatoes, and when cool pour the potato water over the cup of flour. Next add the dissolved yeast, sugar, salt, ginger, and the mashed potatoes. Mix well, and add cornmeal enough to stiffen. Let rise, then shape in bulk, and cut oblong cakes.

MRS. WM. WEYRICH.

Biscuits.

1 qt. of flour; 1 tablespoonful of salt; 1 teaspoonful of baking powder; 1 large spoonful of butter or lard; 1 level teaspoonful of soda; about ½ qt. of buttermilk or sour milk.

These biscuits must be quickly made, not worked.

MRS. P. ROEDER.

Biscuits.

3 cups flour; 2 heaping teaspoonfuls baking powder; ½ teaspoonful salt; 3 tablespoonfuls lard; ½ teaspoonful soda, dissolved in a cup of sour or buttermilk. Use more milk if necessary.

Roll out, cut, and bake in a hot oven.

MRS. LOUIS DIETZ.

Corn Bread.

2 cups corn-meal; 3 eggs; 2 cups boiling water; 2 cups sour milk; 2 tablespoonfuls lard; 1 teaspoonful soda.

Scald corn meal with boiling water and mix in other ingredients.

MRS. H. CORDES.

Corn Bread.

2 cups of sifted meal; ½ cup of flour; 2 cups of buttermilk or sour milk; 2 eggs; 1/3 cup of sugar; 1 teaspoonful of salt; 2 tablespoonfuls of melted butter.

Mix the meal and flour smoothly and gradually add the milk, then the butter, sugar and salt, then the beaten eggs and lastly dissolve a level teaspoonful of baking soda in a little milk and beat thoroughly together. Bake in a quick oven. This recipe can be made with sweet milk by using baking powder.

MRS. W. J. JUNG.

Corn Bread.

2 cups of corn meal, 1 cup of flour, 2½ cups of milk, 3 eggs, 2 tablespoons of butter, 1 tablespoon of sugar, 1 teaspoon of salt, 2 teaspoons of baking powder.

Melt the butter and stir into the eggs, which should have been beaten very light, and after sifting the salt, sugar and baking powder with the meal and flour,, put in the milk, eggs and butter. Beat hard and bake for half an hour in a steady oven.

MRS. ELLA SCHMIDT.

German Coffee Cake.

1½ ℔ flour; ¼ ℔ sugar; ½ ℔ butter; 1 cup raisins; 5 eggs; 1 pt. yeast; grated lemon to flavor.

Mix the above ingredients well and set in a warm place to rise. When well risen make in loaves, put in well greased pans and let rise again; then bake in moderate oven.

MRS. M. PUHL.

Rolls.

½ cup butter; 1 small cup sugar; 3 cups flour; sifted twice with two small teaspoonfuls of baking powder; ½ cup milk; rind of 1 lemon.

Cream butter, eggs and sugar; add flour, then milk. Form into small rolls and paint with beaten egg.

MRS. I GLATZLE.

Plain Coffee Cake.

6 tablespoonfuls of sugar; 1 tablespoonful melted butter; 2 eggs; ½ cup milk; 1 cup raisins, and enough flour to make a medium stiff dough. At night set one yeast cake with a pint of water and ¾ sieve flour at about 10 o'clock and let rise until morning; add sugar, a pinch of salt, eggs, butter and milk, beating well all the while. Then add flour. Set aside to rise, when risen to double its size beat down, put in raisins. Let rise again to former height, brush with melted butter, sprinkle with sugar and cinnamon. This quantity will yield one large or two medium loaves.

MRS. ROBERT BLUM.

Doughnuts.

1 cup sugar; 1 teaspoon salt; 1 cup milk; 1 teaspoon grated orange peel; 2 eggs; 3 teaspoons baking powder; 1 tablespoon butter.

Mix with flour like soft bread dough, roll out one inch thick, cut into rings, let rise until light, then fry in hot lard.

IDA HENNERSDORF.

Doughnuts.

1½ cups yeast; ½ cup butter; 3 eggs; 1½ cups sugar; 1 cup milk; 1 teaspoonful lemon extract; flour enough to make a soft dough.

Let rise, roll out and fry in smoking hot lard.

MRS. RICHARD HENKE.

Doughnuts.

2 cups sugar; 2 eggs; 1 pt. milk; 1 teaspoon salt; 1 qt. flour; 1 grated nutmeg; 3 teaspoonfuls Royal Baking Powder.

Beat well both sugar and eggs, add milk and flour into which the baking powder has been measured. Flour must be added until the dough can be handled. Roll out ½ inch thick, cut in rings or small balls and fry a rich golden brown in a deep kettle of smoking hot fat.

MRS. ED. OEHLER.

Doughnuts.

3 eggs; 3 tablespoons lard; 1 teaspoon nutmeg; 1¼ cups sour cream; 1 1/3 cups sugar; 5 cups flour; 2 teaspoons salt; 1½ teaspoons soda.

Beat whole eggs very lightly, add sugar gradually, beating constantly, add lard and continue beating. Mix and sift flour, nutmeg, salt and soda. Add flour and sour cream alternately. Chill dough, then toss on a slightly floured board; roll ½ inch thick and fry in deep lard.

MRS. AUG. GOLD.

Doughnuts.

1 cup sugar; 2 eggs; ½ cup milk; 1 sifter flour; ½ cup sour cream; 2 teaspoonfuls baking powder.

Cut with biscuit cutter and fry in deep lard.

MRS. A. STAATS.

Love Knots.

½ cup well beaten eggs; ½ cup sweet cream; beat together, and mix stiff with flour, roll out very thin, then cut in two inch squares. These cut in five strips, but not quite through, leave the sides together. Then take in hand, slip each strip under the other, when last one in hand, drop carefully into hot lard and bake a rich golden brown, take out and sprinkle with powdered sugar.

MRS. F. STEIN.

Apple Fritters.

1 cup of flour mixed with 1 teaspoonful baking powder; add 1 cup of milk with yolk of 2 eggs stirred in; add 1½ cups chopped apples; last of all add the whites of 2 eggs beaten very light; drop with spoon into very hot lard. Any fruit can be used.

MRS. E. C. HANSEN.

Graham Gems.

3 cups graham flour; 1 cup white flour; 2 eggs; 1 heaping tablespoon melted butter; 2 tablespoons molasses; 1 teaspoon salt; 2 teaspoons baking powder; 2 cups milk or water.

Do not make dough too stiff. Bake in quick oven in gem pans.

GERTRUDE WEHMEYER.

Cinnamon Roll.

Make a good biscuit dough, roll thin, then spread on the following mixture.

Cream ½ pound butter with 1 cup sugar; spread this on the dough; sprinkle with cinnamon; roll, cut in slices, put in bread pan, add enough water to make juicy while cooking, serve hot with sweet milk or cream.

MRS. ED. WINKEL.

Parker House Rolls.

1 cake Fleischmann's yeast; 1 pint milk scalded and cooled; 2 tablespoons sugar; 4 tablespoons lard or butter melted; 3 pints flour; 1 teaspoon salt. Dissolve yeast and sugar in lukewarm milk, add lard or butter and 1½ pints of flour. Beat until perfectly smooth. Cover and let rise in a warm place 1 hour or until light. Then add remainder of flour or enough to make a stiff dough; add the salt. Knead well and place in a greased bowl. Cover and let rise in a warm place about 1½ hours or until double in bulk. Roll out ¼ inch thick. Brush lightly with melted butter, cut with a 2 inch biscuit cutter, crease through center heavily with dull edge of knife and fold over in pocket book shape. Place in well greased, shallow pans 1 inch apart. Cover and let rise until light about ¾ hour. Bake ten minutes in hot oven.

MRS. WM. HABENICHT.

COOKIES.
Anise Seed Cookies.

½ lb sugar; ½ lb flour; 4 eggs; 1 tablespoon anise seed.

Drop in pan with teaspoon.

MRS. HENRY HENKE, SR.

Anise Cookies.

9 eggs; whites beaten separately; 2 lb of sugar; 4 teaspoons ground anise seed; 2 teaspoons baking powder. Beat the sugar and eggs ½ an hour or more. Then add enough flour to roll out. Cut with tins, put on board until next day. Then bake in a moderate oven.

MRS. FRANK PETERMANN.

Almond Cookies.
(Mandel - Kraenze.)

¾ lb butter, creamed; 3 yolks of eggs; ½ lb sugar; 1 lb flour.

Cut with large round cutter and take out center with a smaller one leaving a circular cookie. Brush these with white of eggs and sprinkle with finely chopped almonds, sugar and cinnamon. Bake a golden yellow in a moderate oven.

MRS. ROEHM.

Cream Puffs.

½ cup butter; 1 cup flour; 1 cup water; 3 eggs;

Let butter and water come to a boil; while boiling stir in the flour; stir until a smooth paste. When cool work in the eggs. Drop on buttered tins and bake in a hot oven about 30 minutes.

FILLING: 1 cup milk, 1 egg, ½ cup sugar; thicken with corn starch, flavor with vanilla.

MRS. M. PUHL.

Brown Cookies.

4 eggs; 1 cup butter; 3 cups brown sugar; 2 cups raisins; 2 cups currants; 1 cup pecans; 6 cups of flour; 4 tablespoons sweet milk, in which dissolve 2 small teaspoons soda.

Flavor to suit your own taste.

MRS. ALFRED LEHNE.

Cream Puffs.

Take a large tablespoon of butter and 1 cupful of water, and put on to boil, then dump into this 1 cupful of sifted flour, stir well until it loosens from the sides, then take from fire, let cool off some, stir in 3 eggs, one after the other, add 1 teaspoon of salt, beat very thoroughly, then let it rest awhile in a cool place, the ice box is best in summer. Then drop in small spoonfuls in pans and bake very thoroughly, or they will fall. When cold cut open, and fill with whipped cream or custard.

MISS MARY STEIN.

Cream Puffs.

Boil with a large cupful of hot water, half a teaspoonful of butter, stirring in one teacupful of flour, during the boiling. Set aside to cool. When cold, stir in 4 unbeaten eggs, one at a time. Drop on tins quickly and bake in a fairly hot oven.

FILLING: 3 tablespoonfuls of flour; 1 egg; 1 teacupful of sugar; stir this into a cupful of milk while boiling. Flavor to taste.   MRS. AUG. CAMERON.

Cookies with Raisins.

1 cup sugar; ½ cup lard; ½ cup sweet milk; 1 beaten egg; 3 cups flour sifted with 3 teaspoonfuls baking powder.

Cream sugar and shortening; add slowly other ingredients; roll out thin, cut out, and place in pan. Put a teaspoonful of the filling on each cookie, place another cookie on top and bake.

For filling mix together ¾ cup sugar; 1 tablespoon flour; 1 cup boiling water; 1 cup raisins, chopped. Cook until thickened.

MRS. C. F. TATSCH.

Cookies.

5 eggs; 1½ cup of sugar; 1 cup of butter or lard; 2 teaspoonfuls of baking powder; flour to make a soft dough.

Extract or spices for flavoring.

IRMA OCHS.

Chocolate Cookies.

1 cupful of sugar; 2 eggs; 7 tablespoonfuls of flour; 1½ teaspoonfuls of baking powder; 1 cupful of chopped pecans; ½ cake sweet chocolate, grated; salt.

Beat eggs lightly, add pinch of salt and sugar; beat again; add flour and baking powder sifted, chocolate and the pecans. Drop little balls on buttered pans and bake slowly.

MRS. OTTO DITTMAR.

Chocolate Cookies.

3 eggs; 1½ cup sugar; 1½ cup flour; 1 teaspoon baking powder; 10c cake German Sweet Chocolate grated. Beat eggs thoroughly and again with the sugar, then add the grated chocolate and lastly flour and baking powder. Drop by spoon on buttered tins and bake in a moderate oven.

MRS. A. WALTER.

Chocolate Jumbles.

2 cups sugar; 1 cup butter; 2 eggs; 1 cup grated chocolate; 3 cups flour; 1 cup nuts; ½ teaspoon baking powder; roll in little balls and bake.

MRS. A. H. KNEESE.

Christmas Cakes.

1 lb flour; ½ lb sugar; ¼ lb butter; 4 eggs.

Sift flour and sugar together, rub in the butter and then the eggs. Roll out very thin, cut in squares and bake.

MRS. HENRY HENKE, SR.

Chocolate Cookies.

2 cups sugar; 1 tablespoonful butter; 3 eggs, beaten separately; 2 cups flour; ½ lb Bakers chocolate; 1 cup pecans; 1 teaspoon baking powder.

MRS. WM. BIERSCHWALE.

Chocolate Cookies.

1 cup chocolate; 1 cup sugar; 1 cup grated cocoanut; 1 cup sweet crackers; 2 eggs; 2 tablespoonfuls butter.

Mix all and drop from spoon on buttered tins; bake in moderate oven.

MRS. H. KALLENBERG.

Date Cookies.

1 cup brown sugar; ¾ cup milk; 1 cup butter or lard; 2 cups oatmeal; 2 teaspoonfuls baking powder; flour enough to roll out.

For filling boil ¾ cup sugar; 1 cup water and 1 lb of dates until smooth, stirring continually. Roll out dough indicated above, cut with cookie cutter, spread Jone cookie with the date-paste, and cover with another round of dough. Bake in moderate oven.

MRS. OTTO KOLMEIER.

Cocoanut Cookies.

1 cup butter; 2 cups sugar; 2 eggs; 1 cup grated cocoanut; 1 teaspoon vanilla; 2 teaspoonfuls baking powder; flour enough to roll out dough.

Bake light brown.

MRS. JOE STEIN.

Cocoanut Cookies.

½ cup butter; 2 eggs; 2 cups sugar; 2 cups cocoanut; 2 cups flour; 1 teaspoon vanilla; ½ teaspoon baking powder.

Drop on buttered tins with a teaspoon.

MRS. EMIL BAETHGE.

Date Kisses.

The whites of 2 eggs; 1 cup powdered sugar; 1 cup rolled pecans; 1 cup chopped dates.

Beat whites of eggs stiff, add sugar and beat again. Then stir in pecans and dates. Drop from teaspoon in buttered pan and bake in a slow oven until delicate brown.

MISS ZULA MAE HILL.

Fruit Cookies.

2 cups sugar; 2 eggs; 1 cup butter; 1 cup raisins; 2 tablespoonfuls sour milk; 1 teaspoonful soda, dissolved in the sour milk; 1 teaspoonful each of nutmeg and cloves; flour enough to roll.

MRS. H. KALLENBERG.
MRS. ALB. STAATS.

Fruit Cookies.

1 cupful of butter; 2 cupfuls of sugar; ½ cupful sweet milk; 3 cupfuls of flour; 3 teaspoonfuls baking powder; 4 eggs; 2 cupfuls of currants; 2 of raisins; 2 of pecans; ½ cup of orange-peel; 1 wine glass of whiskey or wine; 2 tablespoonfuls each of cinnamon and all kinds of spices.

Make up as any cake, flouring the fruit as for fruit cake. Make a stiff batter and drop on pan from spoon. These little cakes are delicious..

MRS. FELIX W. MAIER.

White Lebkuchen.

1 ℔ sugar; 4 eggs; 2 cupfuls pecans; ¼ teaspoonful of cloves; ½ teaspoonful nutmeg.

Stir sugar and eggs for one half hour (adding one egg at a time); then add cloves, nutmeg and pecans, also flour enough to make the dough stiff enough to roll out and cut. Bake a light brown.

MRS. W. J. JUNG.

Hermits.

1 cup of butter; 1½ cups of sugar; 3 eggs; ½ cup of molasses; 1 teaspoonful soda; 1 cup of each, raisins and currants; 1 cup pecans; 1 teaspoonful of each ginger, cloves, cinnamon and allspice; flour enough to roll out soft.

MRS. ED. OEHLER.

Hermits.

2 cups of sugar; 1 cup of butter; 1 cup of stoned and chopped raisins; 3 eggs; ½ teaspoonful of soda,

dissolved in 3 tablespoonsful of milk; 1 nutmeg; 1 teaspoonful of cloves and cinnamon; 5 cups of flour.

MRS. W. H. KUSENBERGER,
MRS. AD. SCHMIDT.

Ginger Snaps.

2 cups sugar; 1 egg; 1 cup molasses; 1 tablespoon ginger; 1 cup butter or lard; 1 cup hot water; 1 teaspoon soda, dissolved in water; flour enough to roll out.

MRS. A. KUENEMANN.

Macaroons.

1 lb finely chopped pecans; 1 lb sugar; unbeaten whites of 4 eggs; grated rind of ½ lemon or a little cinnamon.

Mix the ingredients, drop by teaspoonfuls on a well greased tin and bake in a moderate oven.

MRS. CHAS. NIMITZ.

Lebkuchen.

1 lb dark brown sugar; ¼ gal. black molasses, ¼ lb butter; ¼ lb citron; ¼ glass whiskey; 1½ lb of pecans; 1½ teaspoonfuls of cooking soda; 1 tablespoonful each of cinnamon, cloves, and allspice; grated rind of 1 orange and 2 lemons; ½ lb of flour to start.

Flour, spices, peeling mixed. Pecans not chopped.

Let molasses come to a boil, melt in butter and sugar, let this cool off, add whiskey and soda, pour over dry part mixing quickly and add flour to make good stiff dough. Let stand until next day. Add flour to roll out, bake and ice.

MRS. ROEHM.

Pecan Macaroons.

1 lb of pecans; ¼ lb citron; ¾ lb sugar; grated peel of one orange; 1 nutmeg; 1 teaspoon cinnamon; whites of 6 eggs; beaten yolks of one; 1 teaspoon baking powder; flour enough to make it roll easily; 1 wine glass brandy.

Brush with yolks before baking.

MRS. HERMAN GOLDSCHMIDT.

Oatmeal Cookies (Without Eggs).

1 cupful sugar; 1 cupful molasses; 1 cupful lard; 3½ cupfuls flour; 4 cupfuls of uncooked oatmeal; 2 teaspoonfuls cinnamon.

Dissolve 2 teaspoonfuls of soda in ½ cup boiling water. Mix well and form small cookies with the hand.

MRS. ALVIN STRIEGLER.

Oatmeal Cookies.

2 cups of sugar; 1½ cups of butter; 1 teaspoonful soda; 1 teaspoonful cinnamon; 2 cups of flour; 2 cups of oatmeal; 2 cups of currants; 4 eggs.

MRS. C. W. Fenge.

Oatmeal Macaroons.

1 cupful of sugar; ½ cupful of butter; mix well. 2 well beaten eggyolks; ½ cup of cocoanut; ½ teaspoonful of soda, dissolved in 1 tablespoonful of hot water; 1 cup of flour; 1 teaspoonful of baking powder. Lastly add the well beaten whites of 2 eggs. Drop from teaspoon on well greased pans. Bake 12 to 15 minutes.

MRS. G. H. HOUY.

Chocolate Macaroons.

12 sweet crackers; 2 cups of sugar; 10c-cake of chocolate; 2 cups of pecans; whites of 6 large or 7 small eggs.

Beat the eggs to a stiff froth, add sugar, grated chocolate, then the finely chopped pecans and the mashed crackers. Drop on buttered paper, with a teaspoon.

MRS. R. G. STRIEGLER.

German Nut Cakes.

¾ lb butter; ½ lb sugar; 1 lb flour; yolks of 3 eggs.

Rub butter and sugar to a cream, add the egg yolks, lastly the flour.

Roll out on board, spread with the beaten whites, some chopped nut meats, cinnamon, and sugar. Cut into squares and bake in quick oven.

MRS. R. L. KOTT.

Oatmeal Cookies.

2 cups sugar; 4 eggs; 1½ cups lard; 3 cups oatmeal; 3 cups flour; ¾ cups raisins, 1 teaspoon cinnamon; ¾ cups currants; 1 teaspoon soda.

MRS. LOUIS OEHLER.

Pecan Cookies.

1 lb sugar; 1 lb flour; 6 eggs; 1 cup pecans; 1 teaspoonful baking powder.

MRS. A. KUENEMANN.

Pfeffer-Nuesse. (Pepper Cookies.)

1 ℔ sugar; 6 eggs; 1 teaspoon cinnamon; 1 teaspoon cloves; 1 pinch black pepper; 1 teaspoon baking powder; flour enough to make a very stiff dough.

Cut out and bake in moderate oven.

MRS. HENRY HENKE, SR.

Pfeffer-Nuesse.
(German Cookies.)

4 eggs; 3 cups flour; 4 teaspoonfuls cinnamon; 2 cups sugar; 1 cup pecans; 2 teaspoonfuls cloves; 2 tablespoons butter; 2 nutmeg; 2 teaspoonfuls baking powder.

MRS. LOUIS OEHLER.

Pecan Cookies.

White of 5 eggs; ½ ℔ of sugar; ½ ℔ of pecans, finely chopped; 1 sweet cracker and a little baking powder.

Beat eggs and sugar to a stiff froth, add the baking powder, mixed with the crumbed cracker, and last the pecans. Drop from spoon on a well preased pan.

MRS. R. BLUM.

Pecan Cookies.

2 cups of sugar; yolks of 10 eggs; 1 teaspoonful of cinnamon; 2 cups of pecans; ½ cup of finely chopped citron; a teaspoonful of baking powder.

Flour enough to make a stiff batter. Drop in pan with a teaspoon.

MRS. R. G. STRIEGLER.

Pecan Cookies.

½ cup of pecans; 1 cup of sugar; 1¼ cups of flour; 1 cake of chocolate; 3 large or 4 small eggs; 1 level teaspoon of baking powder; 1 teaspoon vanilla and spices.

Bake in shallow long tins, when done cut into any shape desired and ice.

MRS. GEORGE WRIGHT.

Springerle.

1 ℔ flour; 4 large eggs; 1 ℔ sugar; butter size of a walnut; enough potash to cover the point of a large knife blade twice (you may take baking powder instead) and anise seed.

Sift flour and sugar. Then stir butter, sugar and eggs and potash (which has been dissolved in a little milk) for 15 minutes. Add the flour as much as will make a stiff dough. Roll out dough until about half as thick as your finger. Sprinkle with flour and press the patterns on the dough, then cut or separate the cakes with a dough cutter and place on a board covered with anise seed, or use anise oil. Keep in a dry place over night and the next morning bake in a moderate oven a light yellow.

MRS. O. W. STRIEGLER.

Sugar Cookies.

2 cups sugar; ½ cup lard; 5 eggs; 2 teaspoonfuls baking powder; flour enough to roll.

ROSA DECHERT.

Rock Cookies.

1½ cups brown sugar; 1 cup butter; 3½ cups flour; 1 cup pecans; 1 cup raisins; ½ lb dates; 4 eggs; 1 teaspoonful cinnamon; 1 teaspoonful soda, dissolved in a little hot water; a pinch of salt.

MRS. A. KUENEMANN,
MRS. WM. BIERSCHWALE.

Sugar Cookies.

1½ cups sugar; 2 eggs; 2 large tablespoonfuls milk; ½ cup butter; 3 cups flour; 1 teaspoonful baking powder; 1 teaspoonful vanilla; sprinkle with sugar.

MRS. A. D. STAHL.

Zimmetsterne. (Very Good.)

1 ℔ sifted sugar; whites of 6 eggs; 1 ℔ almonds; 1/8 oz. cinnamon; grated rind of 1 lemon.

The almonds should be washed, dried, and then grated with the brown skin left on. Stir the sugar and lemon peel into the beaten whites of the eggs and continue beating for 15 minutes, then add the cinnamon. Reserve a small part of this mixture for top of cakes, then to the large portion add the almonds. Roll out about 1/8 inch in thickness, using only as much flour as necessary. Cut with star shaped cutter, brush each cookie with the reserved white of egg mixture and bake slowly on well greased pans.

MRS. ROEHM.

Small Tea Cakes.

5 eggs; 1½ cups sugar; 1 cup butter or lard; 2 teaspoonfuls baking powder; spices or extract.

The dough must be worked lightly, rolled out, cut with a cake-cutter and baked in a moderately hot stove.

IRMA OCHS.

Wiener Zollen.

2 cups sugar; 4 eggs; 1 cup pecans; 1 nutmeg; 1 teaspoon cinnamon; ½ teaspoonful cloves; 1½ teaspoon baking powder; enough flour to make a stiff dough, cut in half moons and sprinkle with sugar.

MRS. F. W. ARHELGER.

Wiener Zollen.

2 cups of sugar; 4 eggs; 1 lemon rind and juice; a little cinnamon and cardamon; ½ cup of finely chopped citron; 1 cup of nut meats; 3 cups of flour; 1 teaspoon baking powder. Roll in sugar. Bake in slow oven.

MRS. WALTER MECKEL.

Molasses Cookies (Christmas.)

1 quart molasses; 1 quart sugar; 1 quart pecans; 1 large spoon of lard; 1 tablespoon of cinnamon; 1 teaspoon of cloves; 1 teaspoon of salt.

Heat sugar and molasses until the molasses has melted, when cool stir in the other ingredients and mix well, then roll and cut into shapes with a knife. Let lay over night. Bake the next morning. Apply icing when cold.

MRS. R. C. LUDWIG.

Buttermilk Cookies.

2 cups sugar; 1 cup butter or lard; 1 cup buttermilk; 1 teaspoon soda; 1 box cocoanut or 1 teaspoon Extract. Flour enough to roll out.

MRS. ELLA SCHMIDT.

White Cookies without Eggs.

2 cups sugar; 1 cup butter and lard mixed; 1 cup sour milk; 1 teaspoon soda; 5 cups flour; roll out thin; sprinkle top with sugar and cinnamon. Bake in a quick oven.

MRS. MAX SCHOENEWOLF.

Butter Cookies.

5 eggs; 2 lb sugar; ¼ lb butter; ¼ lb lard, 2 teaspoons baking powder; 1 teaspoon vanilla. Flour enough to roll out. Cut in squares and bake in quick oven.

MRS. FRANK PETERMANN.

Vanilla Wafers.

Cream 1/3 cup shortening (using butter and lard in equal proportion or all butter) and add gradually while beating constantly, one cup sugar, then add 1 egg well beaten, ¼ cup milk and 2 teaspoons vanilla. Mix and sift two cups flour, two teaspoons baking powder and ½ teaspoon salt. Add to first mixture, roll out on a floured board as thinly as possible shape with a small round cutter. Place on buttered tins and bake in a moderate oven.

MRS. WM. HABENICHT.

Lebkuchen.

2 cups sugar; 1 cup butter; 8 eggs, the whites of two of them kept back for icing; 1 cup molasses; 1½ plate German Sweet Chocolate; ½ cup of cut citron; 1 cup cut almonds; 1 cup pecans; 3 cups flour; 2 heaping teaspoonfuls baking powder; 1 teaspoonful of each cinnaman, cloves, allspice, nutmeg.

This is to be baked in an 18 inch pan, when cool cut into 2 inch squares and cover with icing.

MRS. R. C. LUDWIG.

Graham Nut Cookies.

Cream 1½ cups sugar and 2/3 cups lard. Add 2 eggs well beaten; 1 teaspoon each of cinnamon, nutmeg and salt; 1 level teaspoon of soda dissolved in ½ cup sour milk; 1 cup nuts chopped fine; 1 cup shredded cocoanut. Stir in 2½ cups sifted graham flour and drop from teaspoon on greased tins.

ELLA EVERS.

Peanut Cookies.

3 tablespoons shortening; ½ cup sugar; 1 egg; ¼ teaspoon salt; ¾ cup peanuts, roasted and chopped fine; 1 cup flour; 2 tablespoons milk; ½ teaspoon soda; juice of ½ lemon.

Cream shortening and sugar, add beaten eggs. Sift flour, salt and soda, add to other ingredients. Then add milk, peanuts and lemon juice. Drop from teaspoon, on greased tins.

MRS. WALTER MECKEL.

Layer Cakes.

Caramel Cake.

1½ cups sugar; ½ cup butter; yolks of 2 eggs; 1 cup water; 2 cups flour; 3 teaspoonfuls cool caramel syrup; 1 teaspoonful vanilla; ½ cup flour; 2 teaspoonfuls baking powder; stiffly beaten whites of 2 eggs.

Mix well the first five ingredients, adding the others as given. The cake may be baked as a layer cake in a moderate oven, and put together with the following filling.

FILLING: 1 cup sugar; ¼ cup water; white of 1 egg; ½ teaspoonful vanilla; 1 teaspoonful caramel syrup.

Boil sugar and water until the syrup spins a thread, add it to the beaten white, continue beating, adding the vanilla and the caramel syrup.

CARAMEL SYRUP: 1 cup sugar; ½ cup boiling water.

Put the sugar in a sauce pan on the fire; stir constantly until it is a brown color, take from the fire, add water, and stir until the sugar is dissilved.

HELENE HANISCH.

Chocolate Cake.

2 cupfuls of sugar; ½ cupful of butter; 1 cupful of milk; yolks of three eggs; whites of two; 2¾ cupfuls of flour; 3 teaspoonfuls of baking powder; ½ cupful of grated chocolate.

Melt chocolate, add half cupful of milk; when thoroughly mixed let cool. Cream sugar and butter, add yolks of the eggs, then the whites, and remaining ½ cup of milk. Add flour with the baking powder, then the chocolate. Bake in three layers.

FILLING: 1 cupful of sugar; 1/3 cupful of milk; 1 tablespoonful of butter; boil 5 minutes. Beat until cool, add 1 teaspoonful of vanilla. Spread between layers.

MRS. A. H. WELGEHAUSEN.

Delicious Chocolate Cake.

8 eggs, the white beaten stiff; 2 cups of sugar; 1 cake of sweet chocolate; 1 cup of butter; 3 cups of flour; 1 cup of milk; 3 teaspoonfuls of baking powder.

Beat the butter and sugar to a cream; add the milk, then flour and beaten whites. Divide into equal parts and into half grate a cake of sweet chocolate. Bake in layers, spread with custard and alternate the dark and white layers.

FOR CUSTARD: 1 tablespoon of butter; 1 pint of milk, let boil together; then stir in 2 eggs, beaten with 1 cup of sugar and 2 teaspoonfuls of corn starch dissolved in a little cold milk; then boil all and spread on cake.

MRS. G. E. WRIGHT.

Devil's Food Cake. No. 1.

PART 1: 1 cup brown sugar; 1 cup grated chocolate; ½ cup sweet milk.

Allow mixture to come to a boil and set aside to cool.

PART 2: 1 cup brown sugar; ½ cup butter; ½ cup sweet milk; 3 yolks of eggs; 2 cups flour; 2 teaspoonfuls baking powder.

Mix in the usual manner and add to part 1, bake in layers and spread with soft chocolate icing.

MISS BERTHA PRIESS.

Devil's Food Cake. No. 2.

2 cupfuls brown or white sugar; ½ cup butter; ½ cup lard; 2 eggs; 1 cup buttermilk; 3 cups flour; 1½ teaspoonfuls cinnamon; ½ teaspoon allspice; ½ cake of ground chocolate, with enough hot water to make ½ cup; ½ teaspoon soda.

Mix all together and bake in four layers. Put together with cooked icing.

MRS. ALVIN STRIEGLER.

Devil's Food Cake. No. 3.

½ cup butter; 1½ cups sugar; 2 eggs; ½ cup sour milk; 1 teaspoon soda; 2 cups flour; 1 teaspoon vanilla; 2 squares of chocolate.

Cream butter and sugar; add the beaten eggs, the soda dissolved in the same milk ,flour, flavoring, and lastly stir into the batter the chocolate dissolved in ½ cup of boiling water. Bake in two layers and put together with white frosting.

MRS. AUG. JORDAN.

Devil's Food Cake (Layer). No. 4.

5 eggs beaten separately; 2 cups sugar; 1 cup butter; 2 cups flour; 1 small cup grated chocolate (bitter), dissolved in boiling water; 1 level teaspoonful of soda.

Mix well the beaten yolks, sugar and butter, then add 1 cup milk. Sift soda and flour together and stir into mixture. Add the chocolate and lastly fold in the whites. Bake in layers and put together with chocolate filling.

CHOCOLATE FILLING: 1 cup sugar; ½ cup sweet milk; 3 tablespoon grated chocolate (bitter); a pinch of salt.

Boil until it will cream, then remove from fire and beat hard till it is thick enough to spread.

MRS. A. D. STAHL.

Pineapple Cake.

1½ cups powdered sugar; ½ cup butter; ½ cup sweet milk; ½ cup cornstarch; 1½ cups flour; 2 teaspoonfuls baking powder.

Mix the butter and sugar to cream, add the milk, then add the flour, cornstarch and baking powder well mixed and sifted, last add the whites of 8 eggs beaten.

FILLING: 1 can of grated pineapple; 1 cup sugar.

Boil to a thick jelly and let cool. Make a boiled icing of 3 cups sugar; ½ cup water and the beaten whites of 3 eggs.

MRS. SCHWARZ.

Graham Cracker Layer Cake.

28 graham crackers, rolled and mixed with 1 teaspoon baking powder; ½ cup butter; 1 cup sugar creamed with butter; 3 eggs, yolks and whites beaten separately; ¾ cup milk; 1 teaspoon vanilla.

Bake 15 minutes.

MRS. MAX BIERSCHWALE.
MRS. G. L. STEBBINS.

Jam Cake.

3 eggs; 1 cup of sugar; ¾ cup of butter; 1½ cups of flour; 1 cup jam; 4 tablespoonfuls sour milk; 1 teaspoonful of soda dissolved in the sour milk.

Adding jam last.

For flavoring a little cinnamon, allspice and nutmeg. Bake in layers.

FILLING: 2 cups of sugar; 2/3 cupful of milk; butter the size of a pecan. Boil 4 minutes, then beat to a soft creamy mixture. MRS. F. MORGAN.

Plain Layer Cake.

1 cup sugar; 1 tablespoon butter; 3 eggs; ½ cup milk; 2 level teaspoonfuls baking powder; 1 cup flour.

Cream butter and sugar, add eggs one at a time, beaten well, then milk, flour and baking powder.

This makes 2 layers. Use any icing preferred.

MRS. ROBERT BLUM.

Plain Layer Cake.

¾ cup butter; 2 cups sugar; (cream butter and sugar); 5 whole eggs (add 2 at a time and beat thoroughly); 1 cup sweet milk; 3 cups flour; 1 teaspoon baking powder and flavor to taste.

LEMON ICING: 2 cups sugar; yolks of 4 to 6 eggs; 1 heaping tablespoonful of butter; 1 heaping tablespoonful of flour; 1 tablespoonful of water; juice of 1½ lemon. Cook in double boiler.

MRS. FELIX KEIDEL.

Layer Cream Cake.

1 cup butter; 4 eggs; 1 cup milk; 3 cups flour; 2 cups granulated sugar; 1 teaspoonful baking powder; 2 cups fresh cream.

Mix the butter, sugar and yolks of the eggs well, then stir in the milk. Add the flour and baking powder, and the well beaten whites last. (Enough for 4 layers.)

FILLING: Whip the cream and stiffen with sugar and put between the layers when they are thoroughly cool.

MRS. WM. WAHRMUND.

Layer Cream Cake.

¾ cup butter; 1½ cup sugar; 3 eggs; 1 cup milk; 2½ cups flour; 2 teaspoons baking powder; 1 teaspoon any kind of flavoring.

Cream butter and sugar, add eggs one at a time, beating well, then milk, flour, baking powder and flavor.

FILLING: Whipped cream sweetened and flavored to taste.

MRS. LOUIS KOTT.

Lemon Jelly Cake.

1½ cups sugar; ½ cup milk; ½ cup butter; 2½ cups flour; 3 eggs; ½ cup pecans; 2 teaspoonfuls baking powder; 1 teaspoonful of extract of lemon.

FILLING: 2 cups sugar; 1 cup pecans; 2 eggs; 2 teaspoonfuls flour; grated rind and juice of 2 lemons; 2 tablespoonfuls water.

Boil until it thickens, add pecans, cool, and spread between layers. E. LOUDON.

Pecan Layer Cake.

4 eggs; ½ lb butter; ½ lb sugar; ½ lb flour; ½ lb pecans; ½ cup milk; 1 teaspoon cinnamon; 2 teaspoons baking powder.

MRS. H. W. BRAEUTIGAM.

Mahogany Cake.

Dissolve 2 oz. of chocolate in 5 tablespoonfuls of boiling water; cream ½ cup butter with 1½ cups sugar. Add to this the beaten yolks of 4 eggs and the cooled chocolate; next ½ cup of sweet milk; 1¾ cups flour, containing 2 rounded teaspoonfuls baking powder; and lastly the beaten whites of 4 eggs. Bake in 3 layers.

FILLING: Cream 3 cups powdered sugar with ½ cup butter; yolk of 1 egg; 2 tablespoonfuls powdered chocolate mixed with 5 tablespoonfuls strong hot coffee; stir well, add 2 teaspoonfuls vanilla and 2 teaspoonfuls cream. Beat until smooth and light. Do not cook this filling.

MRS. LOUIS DURST.

Orange Cake.

½ cup butter; 1 cup sugar; ½ cup milk; 1½ cups flour; 3 eggs (whites only); ¾ teaspoonful baking powder.

Cream butter and sugar well, beat whites of eggs and add alternately with flour, baking powder and milk to the creamed butter and sugar.

FILLING: 1 orange; ½ lemon; ¾ cup milk; 3 eggs; 3 tablespoonfuls sugar; ½ tablespoonful butter; 1 tablespoonful flour; a pinch of salt.

Mix the flour with a little of the cold milk, stir into the boiling milk and let boil a few minutes. Remove from stove and add the juice and grated rind of 1 orange and the juice of ½ lemon, and yolks of 3 eggs.

MRS. HUGO BORGFELD.

One Egg Cake.

1 heaping tablespoon butter; 1 cup sugar; 1 egg; 1 cup milk; 2 cups flour; 2 teaspoons baking powder; 1 teaspoon extract. Bake in pan or in two layers.

ICING: 1 cup milk; 1 cup sugar; ¾ cup cocoanut; ½ teaspoon vanilla.

MRS. WERNER KEIDEL.
MRS. ALFRED HENKE.

Plain Cocoanut Layer Cake.

1 cup sugar; ½ cup milk; 3 tablespoonfuls butter; 1 cup flour; 2 level teaspoonfuls of baking powder; 1 teaspoon vanilla; 4 eggs.

Cream butter and sugar, add eggs one at a time, then milk and flour into which baking powder has been sifted. This quantity makes 2 layers.

ICING: Beat 2 whites of eggs to a stiff froth; add six tablespoonfuls sugar, spread on layers, sprinkle with cocoanut and set into stove to brown.

MRS. ROBERT BLUM.

Spice Cake.

4 eggs, reserving the whites of 2; 2 cups of brown sugar; ½ cup of melted butter; ½ cup of sour milk; 1 teaspoonful of soda; 2 teaspoonfuls of cinnamon; 1½ teaspoonfuls of cloves; ½ teaspoonful of nutmeg; 2 cups of flour.

Dissolve the soda in the sour milk. Bake in layers.

Make the icing to spread between layers, with the whites of the eggs and 1 cup of sugar.

MRS. LOUIS OEHLER.

Sponge Cake.

3 eggs; 1 cup sugar; 3 tablespoons water; 1 cup flour; 1 teaspoon baking powder.

Beat eggs separately, then add sugar and water, then add flour with baking powder.

This makes 2 layers.

MRS. ALFRED LEHNE.

Strawberry Short Cake.

2 cups of flour; 1/4 cup of butter; 1 teaspoon baking powder.

Sift flour and baking powder several times, then put in the butter and mix well with fingers. Now add milk enough to make a dough, stiff to roll.

Bake in a very hot oven. When done split cake horizontally, and butter both parts well. Now spread the lower part with berries and sugar, put on the top and dust with powdered sugar.

Serve with crushed berries and cream.

Peaches and other fruits may be used with this cake.

MRS. AD. WEHMEYER.

White Layer Cake.

1/2 cup butter, creamed with 1 cup sugar; 1/2 cup milk; 1 3/4 cups flour; 1 1/2 teaspoonfuls baking powder; 3 whites of eggs, stiffly beaten.

Bake in moderate oven in 3 layers.

FILLING: Boil 2 cups of sugar with 1 cup of water until it threads from a fork. Pour over the stiffly beaten whites of two eggs; add 1 cup of chopped pecans and 1 cup of raisins.

MRS. LOUIS DURST.

White Cocoanut Cake with Yellow Filling.

The whites of 4 eggs beaten to a stiff froth, 1½ cupful of sugar; 1 cupful of sweet milk; 3 teaspoonfuls of baking powder and flour enough to make a moderately stiff dough. Bake in layers.

FILLING: Take ½ cupful of sugar and 1 tablespoon of water; let dissolve and then boil till its threads. Add the yolks of 4 eggs, well beaten, and the juice of 2 oranges. Spread between the layers, sprinkle cocoanut on top. (¼ of a lemon may be used instead of the oranges.)

MRS. EDNA ALSTON.

White Layer Cake.

Whites of 6 eggs; 2 cups of sugar; ¾ cup of butter; 1 cup of sweet milk; 3 cups of flour; 2 teaspoonfuls of baking powder.

Cream sugar and butter, then add flour sifted twice with baking powder; add milk and when mixed, add the whites of eggs beaten to a stiff froth. Beat thoroughly and bake in four layers.

FILLING: ¾ cup milk; 2 cups sugar; the whites of 2 eggs; ½ cup pecans; raisins and currants.

Boil milk and sugar till it forms a soft ball when dropped in cold water. Have ready the whites of eggs beaten stiff and pour syrup over them, beating well till cool. Then add pecans, raisins and currants and spread between layers.

MISS ALVINA GOLD.

Wedding Cake. (Braut-Torte.)

1 cup butter; 1 cup chopped pecans; 1 cup sugar; 6 eggs; 1 teaspoon baking powder; vanilla flavor; 2¼ cups flour; 2 to 3 spoons water.

Cream butter and sugar, add yolks of eggs, water, pecans, finally whites of eggs and flour in which baking powder has been sifted alternately. Bake in hot oven, in four layers.

FILLING: ¼ ℔ butter; ¼ ℔ sugar; 4 yolks of eggs; juice of 4 lemons. Beat over fire constantly. Ice cake with cooked icing.

MRS. FRITZ KNUST.
MRS. O. W. STRIEGLER.

Cracker Cake.

4 eggs; 2 cups of sugar; ½ cup butter; 1 cup of milk; 1 cup of soda crackers; 1 cup of pecans; 1 cup flour; 1 teaspoonful of extract; 1½ teaspoonful of baking powder.

ICING: 1 cup hot water; 1 cup sugar; yolk of 1 egg; 1 lemon; 1 tablespoonful cornstarch; 1 teaspoonful butter.

MRS. ALFRED HENKE.

Cocoanut Layer Cake.

3 eggs; 1 cup sugar; 2 tablespoons butter; 2 teaspoons baking powder; 1 cup sweet milk; 2 cups sugar.

WHITE FILLING: 2 cups sugar; ¾ cup sweet milk. Cook 5 minutes, then add 1 teaspoon butter and 1 teaspoon flavoring. Take from oven and beat till creamy. Spread on cake quickly before it hardens.

MRS. EMIL KOLMEIER.

Illinois Cake.

5 eggs; 2 cupfuls of sugar; 1 cupful of butter; 2 teaspoonfuls of baking powder; 3 cupfuls of flour, and 1 cupful of sweet milk. Flavor with vanilla.

FILLING: 1 cupful of sugar and enough water to dissolve the sugar; put in a pan and let simmer on the stove until it candies. Then chop fine, 1 cupful of seedless raisins. Stir into the candied sugar, then add the beaten whites of 2 eggs; flavor with vanilla.

MRS. AD. GOLD.

Lady Baltimore Cake.

1 cup butter; 2 cups sugar; 1 cup milk; 3½ cups flour; whites of 3 eggs; 1 teaspoon rose water; 3 teaspoons baking powder.

FILLING: 3 cups sugar; 1 cup boiling water; 1 cup chopped raisins; 1 cup nut meats; 5 figs, cut in thin slices, whites of 3 eggs.

MRS. WM. KUENEMANN.

Potato Cake.

1 cup butter; 2 cups sugar; 4 eggs; 1 cooked potato; ½ cup sweet milk; 1 cup chopped pecans; ½ cup chocolate; 1 teaspoon cinnamon; ½ teaspoon cloves; ½ teaspoon nutmeg; 2 cups flour; 2 teaspoons baking powder.

CHOCOLATE CARAMEL FILLING: ½ lb sugar; ¼ lb grated chocolate; ½ cup sweet milk; butter, size of an egg. Mix and cook to a syrup stiff enough to spread.

MRS. AUG. JORDAN.

Potato Cake.

2½ cups of sugar; ½ cup of butter; ½ cup of potatoes, (mashed); ½ cup of milk; ½ cup of grated chocolate; 2½ cups of flour sifted with 2 heaping teaspoons baking powder; ½ teaspoon cinnamon; 5 eggs; 1 cup pecans. Bake in three layers.

FILLING: 2 cups sugar; 2/3 cup milk; butter the size of a pecan. Boil for 4 minutes, then add ½ cup pecan meats; ½ cup raisins; ½ teaspoon vanilla. Beat until creamy.   MRS. ELLA SCHMIDT.
                                 MRS. WM. KALLENBERG.

Frosting for Angel Food.

1 cup of sugar; ¼ cup of milk; a small piece of butter; 1 teaspoon of vanilla.

Dampen sugar with the milk. Stir till it dissolves and boil. Then let it boil about five minutes, not longer; remove from fire, set in a dish containing cold water, add flavor. Stir till it stiffens, then spread quickly on cake as it hardens rapidly.

MRS. EMIL RILEY.

Marshmallow Frosting.

2 tablespoonfuls of milk; 6 tablespoonfuls sugar; ½ teaspoon vanilla; ¼ lb marshmallows; 2 tablespoonfuls hot water.

Heat 2 tablespoonfuls of milk with 6 tablespoonfuls sugar, and boil 6 minutes without stirring. In a double boiler, heat ¼ lb marshmallows and when very soft, add 2 tablespoonfuls of hot water. Cook until smooth. Beat into it the hot syrup (boiled milk and sugar) and beat well until cool. Use at once.

MRS. EMIL RILEY.

Marshmallow Filling.

2 cups sugar; ½ cup water; ½ ℔ marshmallows; 2 eggs.

Boil sugar and water till it ropes. Add the marshmallows broken in small bits. When these have dissolved, pour gradually into the beaten whites of 2 eggs. Beat until cold and spread on cake.

MRS. HERMAN USENER.

Simple Cake Frosting, uncooked.

White of 1 egg; 2 cups powdered sugar; butter, size of walnut; vanilla flavoring.

Put unbeaten white of egg in bowl. Add sugar gradually till paste is smooth. Then add butter (soft but not melted), and vanilla.

MRS. G. L. STEBBINS.

Boiled Frosting.

1 cup granulated sugar; ¼ cup boiling water; ½ teaspoon cream of tartar; white of 1 egg.

Put sugar and water in pan on stove and stir till sugar dissolves. Add cream of tartar and do not stir again. Beat egg white stiff. Cook syrup until it spins. Beat into whipped egg. A pinch of salt and any desired flavoring may be used.

MRS. G. L. STEBBINS.

Orange Icing.

Boil 2 cupfuls sugar; 1 cupful water, until it strings. Pour over well beaten yolks of 4 eggs; beat until smooth and thick; add 1½ teaspoonfuls orange extract, and spread rapidly on cake.

MISS OLGA VON HAGEN.

Chocolate Cake Frosting.

2 cups powdered sugar; 1 teaspoon butter; 1 teaspoon vanilla; 1 1/3 oz. chocolate, some grated orange peel. To the sugar add enough boiling water to make a smooth paste, then add the other ingredients and spread on cake.

MRS. MAX SCHOENEWOLF.

Devils Food Layer Cake.

4 eggs; 1 cup butter; 1 cup white sugar; 1 cup brown sugar; 1 cup molasses; 1 cup sweet milk; 1/2 cup boiling water; 2 cups chopped nuts; 1/2 cup citron; 2 cups raisins; 1 teaspoon cream of tartar; 1/2 teaspoon soda; 1 teaspoon each of allspice, cloves, cinnamon, and nutmeg. Flour enough to make a stiff batter.

Bake in layers and put together with filling.

CHOCOLATE CARAMEL FILLING: 2 cups sugar; 1/2 cup grated chocolate; 1/2 cup sweet milk; butter the size of an egg. Mix and cook to a syrup thick enough to spread.

MRS. MATTIE B. HARRIS.

Crumb Layer Cake.

2 cups flour; 2 eggs; 3/4 cup butter; 1 cup milk; 1 1/2 cups sugar; 2 teaspoonfuls baking powder.

Crumb flour, baking powder, sugar and butter, then add milk and eggs.

Makes three large layers.

MRS. WALTER KLAERNER.

LOAF CAKES

Angel's Food Cake.

Whites of 11 eggs; 1½ cups sugar; 1 cup of flour; 1 teaspoon cream of tartar; flavoring.

To the stiffly beaten whites of eggs add the sugar, then gradually the flour and cream of tartar sifted together. Flour should be sifted five times. Bake in an ungreased pan in a moderate oven 45 minutes.

MRS. AUG. JORDAN.

Angel's Food Cake.

1 cup sugar, sifted 3 times; 1¼ cups flour; 3 teaspoonfuls baking powder; a pinch of salt; whites of 2 eggs, beaten stiffly; 1 cupful milk; vanilla flavoring.

Heat milk and pour over dry ingredients, well sifted, add vanilla and carefully fold in whites of eggs. Bake in moderate oven 35 minutes.

MRS. H. W. KUSENBERGER.

Arch Angel Cake.

1 cup butter; 1 cup sugar; 2 cups sifted flour; 1 teaspoon baking powder; whites of 8 eggs; 1 teaspoon vanilla.

Cream butter and sugar, add flour sifted with baking powder, stir in beaten whites and vanilla and bake. This can be baked in layers with marshmallow filling.

MRS. A. L. PATTON.

Apple Cake.

One cup sugar; 1 of milk; 1 egg; 1 tablespoon butter; 2 even teaspoons baking powder sifted in 2 cups of flour. If dough is too thin, add more flour. Peel and slice enough apples to cover the cake. Put the dough in pan and put apples on as for pie. Sprinkle with sugar and cinnamon and bake in a hot oven. Simple, but very delicious.

MRS. WM. DIETEL.

Apple Sauce Cake. (without Eggs.)

½ cup lard, butter may be substituted; 1 cup sugar; 2 cups flour; 1 cup apple sauce. Cook fresh apples or dried apples until tender without sugar; press through fruit press. Stir 1 teaspoonful soda, (dissolved in 3 tablespoons of hot water,) into the apple sauce; add this to the well stirred shortening and sugar; then add 1 cup raisins; 1 cup pecans; 1 teaspoonful each of cinnamon, cloves, nutmeg and vanilla flavor. Add flour last. Bake slowly.

MRS. EMIL TOEPPERWEIN.
Menard, Texas.

Almond Cake.

15 eggs; ¾ lb sugar; ¾ lb almonds; grated rind of 1 lemon and 1 orange.

Beat yolks and sugar at least 15 minutes; add almonds ground unblanched, lastly the well beaten whites of the 15 eggs. Bake ¾ of an hour in moderate oven.

MRS. EUGENE VANDER STUCKEN.

Cup Cake.

4 eggs; 1 cup butter; 2 cups sugar; 3 cups flour; 1 cup sweet milk; 2 teaspoons baking powder.

Flavor to taste.

MRS. A. L. PATTON.

Brides Cake.

3 cups of sugar; 1 cup of butter; 1 cup of sweet milk; 5 cups of flour; ½ cup of cornstarch; whites of 14 eggs; 2 teaspoonfuls of baking powder; 1 teaspoon each of lemon and vanilla extract.

Stir sugar and butter to a cream, mix milk and cornstarch, then mix together and put in the whites well beaten and flour sifted several times.

MRS. H. CORDES.

Coffee Cake.

1 cup coffee; 1 cup molasses; 1 cup butter; 1 cup sugar; 1 cup raisins; 1 cup currants; 4 cups flour; 1 nutmeg; ½ teaspoon cinnamon; ½ teaspoon cloves; 4 eggs; ½ teaspoon soda, dissolved in hot water.

MRS. A. L. PATTON.

Quick Coffee Cake.

¼ cup butter; 1 cup sugar, creamed together; 1 beaten egg; ½ cup milk; ¼ teaspoonful salt; 1½ cups flour; 1 teaspoon baking powder.

Turn into a well buttered shallow pan, pour over top 2 tablespoonfuls melted butter, sprinkle thickly with sugar and cinnamon, bake in a quick oven.

MRS. LOUIS DURST.

Crumb Cake.

2 cups flour; 2 eggs; ¾ cup butter; ¾ cup milk; 1½ cups sugar; 2 teaspoonfuls baking powder.

Crumb flour, butter, sugar and baking powder. Reserve ½ cup of this mixture; add the eggs and milk. Put in buttered pan, sprinkle with remaining half cup of mixture, and bake in a moderate oven.

MRS. M. PUHL.

Date and Nut Loaf.

1 lb of stoned dates; 1 lb of nuts; 1 cup of sugar; 1 cup of flour; 4 eggs, beaten separately; 2 teaspoonfuls of baking powder; 1 teaspoonful of vanilla; ½ teaspoonful of salt.

Cream yolks of eggs and sugar, sift baking powder and salt into flour, stir into mixture, then fold in the beaten whites lightly, add vanilla and drop in dates and nuts a few at a time; stir well, then drop all in a loaf pan and bake slowly one hour.

MRS. G. E. WRIGHT.

Cup Cake.

1 cup of butter; 2 cups of sugar; 3 cups of flour; 1 cup of milk; 1 cup of raisins; 1 cup of currants; 1 cup of pecans; 2 teaspoonfuls of baking powder; 4 eggs; ½ teaspoonful of allspice; rind of one lemon.

Bake one hour.

MISS IRMA OCHS.

Chocolate Molasses Cake.

6 yolks of eggs; whites of two; 1 cup brown sugar; 1 cup molasses; 1 cup pecans; 7 squares of sweet chocolate; 3 cups of flour; 1 teaspoon baking powder; a small piece of citron; knife point each of cloves, cinnamon and allspice.

Mix well, bake in a bread pan, and cut in squares when baked.

MRS. EMIL WEBER.

Fruit Cake.

1 ℔ butter; 1 lb sugar; 6 eggs; orange and lemon peel; 1 glass wine; 1 glass brandy; ¼ ℔ cocoa; ¼ ℔ cherries (sugared); ½ cup molasses; ½ cup sour milk; 1 teaspoon soda; 1 teaspoon of allspice, cinnamon and cloves; 1 teaspoon ginger; 2 teaspoons baking powder; 1 ℔ raisins; 1 ℔ currants; ½ ℔ pecans; ¼ ℔ citron; ½ ℔ figs; ½ ℔ dates; ¼ ℔ almonds (or other kinds of fruit desired); flour enough to stiffen.

MRS. ARNOLD KOTT.

Citron Pound Cake.

¾ ℔ butter; 1 ℔ sugar; 8 eggs; 1 ℔ flour; 1¼ ℔ citron.

Cream the butter and sugar. Add beaten yolks of eggs and the flour. Add the beaten whites of eggs, then the finely chopped citron, lightly dredged with flour. Bake 1½ to 2 hours.

MRS. HERMAN USENER.

Fruit Cake. (Prize Cake.)

12 eggs; 1 pound sugar; 1 pound butter; 1 pound pecans; 1 pound currants; 1 pound raisins; 1 pound dates or figs; ¼ pound citron; ¼ pound lemon and orange peeling; 1 large apple; 1 grated nutmeg; 1 wine glass of brandy; 1 teaspoonful of cinnamon; ½ teaspoonful of cloves; ½ teaspoonful of mace; ½ teaspoonful of allspice; 1 pound of flour; 2 teaspoonfuls of baking powder; a pinch of salt.

Cream together butter and sugar to a paste, adding the well beaten yolks, then all the fruit, spices and brandy, flour and baking powder, lastly adding the whites of the eggs, well beaten.

Bake two or three hours.

MISS META DIETZ.

Cup Fruit Cake.

¾ cup butter; 2 cups sugar; 1 cup milk; 3 eggs; 3 cups flour; 1 cup nuts; 1 cup raisins; 3 level teaspoonfuls baking powder.

ROSA DECHERT.

Devil's Food Cake.

PART 1. 1 cup brown sugar; ½ cup butter; ½ cup sweet milk; yolks of 3 eggs; 2 cups flour; 1 teaspoon soda.

PART 2. ½ cup cocoa; 1 cup brown sugar; ½ cup sweet milk; 1 teaspoon vanilla.

Boil and when cool mix with part 1. Bake in slow oven.

MRS. WM. BIERSCHWALE.

Potato Fruit Cake.

2 cups of sugar; ½ cup of butter; 4 eggs; 1 cup of warm mashed potatoes; 4 ounces of bitter chocolate; ¾ cup of water; 1 teaspoonful of cinnamon; ½ teaspoon of mace; 2 cups of flour; 3 teaspoons baking powder; ½ cup of raisins; ½ cup of nuts; ½ cup of currants.

Cream butter, sugar and yolks of eggs, add chocolate and spices, then add potatoes and flour and water alternately, and lastly the whites of eggs and fruit. Bake one hour.

MRS. A. H. WELGEHAUSEN.

White Fruit Cake.

1 cup butter; 2 cups sugar; 3 to 3½ cups flour, sifted 4 times; 2 teaspoons baking powder; 1 cup sweet milk; whites of seven eggs; Flavor with lemon extract, and 1/3 cup of wine. (Wine may be omitted); 1 ℔ Sultana raisins; ½ ℔ pecan meats; ½ ℔ almonds, blanched; ½ ℔ candied cherries and ½ ℔ candied pineapple; 1 fresh grated cocoanut. Cut fruit fine and flour well. Bake two hours or more in slow oven.

MRS. F. W. ARHELGER.
MRS. P. W. LEMONS.

Fruit Cake (without Eggs.)

½ cup of sugar; ½ cup of molasses; 1 cup sour milk; 1 cup seeded raisins; 4 tablespoonfuls butter; 1 teaspoonful each of cinnamon, cloves, nutmegs and soda; 2 cups of flour and nuts if desired.

MRS. AD. SCHMIDT.

President's Fruit Cake. (Very Good.)

1 ℔ butter; 1 ℔ sugar (brown); 1 ℔ flour (browned and sifted 3 times); 12 eggs beaten separately; 5 ℔ seeded raisins; 1½ ℔ shredded citron peel; 1 ℔ crystallized cherries; 1 ℔ crystallized diced pineapple; 1 ℔ pecans; 1 ℔ blanched almonds cut fine; 1 glass grape jelly; 2 teaspoonfuls melted chocolate; 1 scant tablespoonful nutmeg; ½ tablespoonful allspice; 1 scant teaspoonful cloves; 1 glass grape juice, and 2 teaspoonful rose water. Soak almonds over night in rose water and fruit in grape juice, cream butter and sugar, add well beaten yolks of eggs, then spices, grape jelly and

chocolate, add whites of eggs, and part of flour, roll fruit in rest of flour, add nuts last bake 4 hours.

MRS. MAX WINKEL.

Old English Fruit Cake.

1 egg; 1 cup molasses; 1 cup buttermilk; 1 cup sugar; 1 cup butter; 2 cups flour; 1 teaspoonful soda; 1 teaspoonful cinnamon; 1 teaspoonful cloves; 1 teaspoonful ginger; 1 nutmeg; ½ lb citron; ½ lb lemon peel; ½ lb orange peel; ½ lb candied pineapple; 1 lb raisins; 1 lb currants; 1 lb dates; 1½ lb pecans.

Dredge spices and fruit with flour and let stand over night.

MRS. G. E. WRIGHT.

Premium Fruit Cake.

3 cups sugar; 1½ cups butter; 6 eggs; 1½ cups sour cream; 2 teaspoonfuls soda; ½ lb currants; ¾ lb raisins; ¼ lb citron; 1 nutmeg; sufficient flour to form stiff batter.

MRS. MOURSUND.

Lightning Cake.

1 cup butter; 4 eggs; 1 cup sugar; 1 heaping cup flour; 1 teaspoonful baking powder; rind and juice of one lemon.

Cream butter and sugar; add beaten eggs, then flour; beat well. Spread 1 inch thick on flat buttered pans, sprinkle with a mixture of sugar and cinnamon. Bake in hot oven; when done cut in squares.

MISS E. LUNGKWITZ.
MRS. ALB. STAATS.

Pecan Cake.

½ cup butter; 1½ cups sugar; ¾ cups milk; 2 cups flour; 2 level teaspoonfuls baking powder; 1 cup nuts (chopped fine); 4 whites of eggs.

Sift flour and baking powder 3 times; cream butter, add sugar, then alternately milk and flour, lastly the whites of the eggs and nut meats. Bake in a sheet in a shallow pan 30 to 40 minutes.

CHOCOLATE ICING: 1 cup sugar; ½ oz. chocolate; 1 white of egg (beaten dry); ¼ cup water; ½ teaspoonful vanilla extract.

Boil sugar, water and chocolate, stirring. Cover vessel and boil 3 minutes. Uncover and boil until it forms a soft ball when tested in cold water; then beat slowly into the white of egg and continue beating (after extract is added) until thickened sufficiently to spread on cakes.

MRS. HENRY HIRSCH.

Pecan Cake. (Nuss Torte.)

1 ℔ pecans, (ground or chopped very fine); 1 ℔ sugar, 12 eggs, (whites of 7 eggs to be beaten separately); 4 tablespoons flour; spices to taste; grated rind of one lemon; a pinch of baking powder.

Beat the 12 egg yolks; 5 whites and sugar, at least 15 minutes. Add the grated lemon rind, spices, pecans, and lastly add alternately the stiffly beaten whites of the 7 eggs, and the flour, sifted with the baking powder. Bake at least one hour in a moderate oven, and do not shake while baking.

MRS. AUG. CAMERON.

Mandelbrot.

1¼ cups chopped almonds or nuts; 2 cups sugar; 1 lb. flour; 4 eggs; teaspoonful cinnamon, cloves, nutmeg; 1 teaspoon baking powder.

Mix dry ingredients well, add eggs, roll out, bake ½ hour. Cut into squares while still warm, then ice.

MRS. FRITZ KNUST.

Nut Cake.

3 eggs; 1½ cups sugar; ½ cup butter; ½ cup milk; 2½ cups flour; 1 cup nut meat; 1½ teaspoonfuls baking powder.

MRS. HENRY BASSE.

Potato Cake. No. 1.

2 cups sugar; 1 cup butter, stir to a cream; 4 well-beaten eggs; ½ cup cooked potatoes; ½ cup grated chocolate; ½ cup milk; 3 cups flour; 1 teaspoonful baking powder; 1 cup pecans; spices to taste.

MISS BERTHA PRIESS.

Potato Cake. No. 2.

1 cup butter; 2 cups sugar; ½ cup milk; 1 cup pecans; 2½ cups flour; 1 cup boiled potatoes, grated; 4 eggs, whites beaten to a froth; 1 nutmeg; 1 teaspoonful cinnamon; ½ teaspoonful cloves; ½ cake chocolate; 2 teaspoonfuls baking powder.

Add grated potatoes last.

MRS. J. A. SCHLEYER.
MRS. A. KUENEMANN.

Reception Cake.

1 cup butter (small); 1½ cups flour; 5 eggs; 1½ cups powdered sugar; 1 teaspoonful baking powder.

Beat butter until creamy; add flour gradually while beating constantly; beat yolks of eggs until lemon colored; add sugar while beating constantly. Combine mixtures and add stiffly beaten whites of eggs. Sift over one teaspoonful of baking powder; beat thoroughly, turn into buttered and flamed dripping pan and bake in moderate oven. When done spread with icing and cut in diamond shaped pieces.

MRS. MOURSUND.

Silver Cake.

2 cups sugar; 3 cups flour; whites of 6 eggs; 2 tablespoonfuls baking powder; 1 cup butter; ¾ cup sweet milk.

Cream well butter and sugar; pour in milk. Stir in alternately the well beaten eggs and the flour which has been sifted several times with the baking powder. Bake in moderate oven.

MISS JULIA H. ESTILL.

Silver Cake.

½ cup of butter; 1½ cups of sugar; 1 cup of milk; 2 cups of flour; 2 teaspoonfuls of baking powder; whites of 5 eggs beaten; ¼ teaspoon flavoring.

Beat thoroughly, before the whites of the eggs are added. The whites are folded in quickly and the cake baked in a moderate oven 1 hour.

MRS. ED. STEIN.

White Cake.

1 cupful of butter; 2 cupfuls of sugar; 3½ cupfuls of flour; 2 teaspoonfuls of baking powder; whites of seven eggs; 1 cupful of milk.

Cream the butter and sugar, add the flour sifted with the baking powder, whites of eggs. Bake one hour.

MRS. E. VANDER STUCKEN.

White Cake.

¾ cup butter; 1 cup milk; 4 egg-whites; 3 cups flour; 1¼ cups sugar; 3 level teaspoons baking powder; 1 level teaspoon salt.

Cream butter and sugar, add milk, then flour, baking powder and salt, which should be sifted thoroughly. Add whites of the eggs last, stirring gently. Use any flavoring to suit taste.

MRS. AUGUSTA FRANZ.

Sunshine Cake. (Prize Cake.)

Whites of 7 eggs; yolks of 5 eggs; 1 cup sugar; 1 cup flour; pinch of salt; ½ teaspoon cream of tartar.

Beat the whites of the eggs to which has been added the pinch of salt. When about half done, add cream of tartar and beat until very stiff. Add sugar, the beaten yolks, and lightly fold in the flour. Bake in ungreased mold from 20 to 40 minutes. Invert into cups and let stand until cold.

MRS. ADOLPH WEBER.

Spice Cake (Without Eggs.)

1 cup sugar; ½ cup butter or lard; 1 teaspoon cinnamon; ½ teaspoon allspice; 1 teaspoon nutmeg; 2 tablespoons chocolate or cocoa; ½ cup pecans; 1 cup raisins; 1 cup sour milk; 1 teaspoon soda dissolved in 2 tablsspoons sour milk; 1 teaspoon vanilla extract; 2¾ cups flour.

MRS. ALFRED GROBE.

Spice Cake.

1 cup of molasses; ½ cup butter; 1 cup of sugar; 2 eggs; 2 teaspoonfuls of vinegar; 2 teaspoonfuls of soda; ½ teaspoonful each of cloves, allspice and cinnamon; ½ cup of strong coffee; flour to make a stiff dough.

Mix all except molasses. Heat molasses and mix in spices, when cool mix all together and bake in quick oven.

MRS. H. CORDES.

Spice Cake. (Layer of Loaf Cake.)

1½ cups sugar; 1 cup butter; 1 teaspoonful of allspice; 1 cup raisins; 1 teaspoonful of cinnamon; 1 cup sour milk; 1 teaspoonful of nutmeg; 3 cupfuls of flour; 2 teaspoonfuls baking powder; 3 eggs.

This cake may also be made in three layers.

MRS. MAX SCHOENEWOLF.

Loaf Sponge Cake.

6 eggs; 1 cup boiling water; ¼ cup cornstarch; ½ teaspoon lemon extract; 2 cups sugar; 2¾ cups flour; 1 teaspoon baking powder.

Beat the yolks of the eggs very light, beating the sugar in gradually. Add the beaten whites of the eggs and the boiling water. Beat in very lightly the flour, cornstarch, and baking powder well sifted together. Flavor. Bake in a loaf pan in a moderate oven.

MRS. FELIX W. MAIER.

Snow Cake.

1 cup butter; 2 cups sugar; 1 cup cornstarch; 2 cups flour; whites of 7 eggs; 1 cup cream; 2 teaspoonfuls baking powder.

Cream the butter and sugar, add cornstarch and the cream, then the flour sifted two or three times with the powder. Beat the whites very stiff and fold into the batter, beating as little as possible after adding eggs. Flavor with lemon extract. MRS. A. D. STAHL.

Gold Cake.

Cream together 1 cup sugar and ¾ cups butter, add 1 whole egg and the yolks of 5 well beaten eggs, then ½ cup milk, 1 teaspoon vanilla and 2 cups of flour into which 1 heaping teaspoon baking powder has been sifted.

Bake in moderate oven.

ELLA NAUWALD SCHAEFER.

Chocolate Cake.

1½ cups sugar ½ cup butter; 2 eggs; ½ cup cocoa; ½ cup hot water; 2 cups flour; ½ cup sour milk; 1 teaspoon soda; 1 teaspoon vanilla.

MRS. EMIL KOLMEIER.

Lunch Cake.

1 cup sugar; ½ cup butter; 1 cup sour milk; 2 cups flour; 1 egg; 1 teaspoon soda; 2 tablespoons molasses; 1 teaspoon cinnamon; ½ teaspoon nutmeg; ½ teaspoon cloves and fruit.

MRS. WM. KALLENBERG.

Poor Man's Cake. (Without Eggs.)

2 cups sugar, 2 tablespoons butter, 2 cups sour milk, 1 tablespoon cinnamon, 1 cup raisins, a little nutmeg, 1 cup nuts, 1 teaspoon cloves, 1 teaspoon soda, 3 cups flour.

Bake in shallow bread pan.

MRS. LEWIS K. SMITH.

Marble Cake. — Light.

1 cup of white sugar, ½ cup of butter, ½ cup of milk, whites of 3 eggs, 2 cups of prepared flour.

Dark.

½ cup of brown sugar, ¼ cup butter, ½ cup molasses, ¼ cup milk, ½ nutmeg, 1 teaspoonful cinnamon, ½ teaspoonful allspice, ½ teaspoonful soda, 2 cups flour, yolks of 3 eggs.

Fill the pan with alternate spoonfuls of light and dark batter. MRS. E. C. HANSEN.

Three Egg Angel Food.

1 cup sugar, 1 1/3 cup flour, ½ teaspoon cream of tartar, 3 teaspoons baking powder, a little salt, 1 teaspoon vanilla, 2/3 cup scalded milk, whites of three eggs.

Mix and sift first five ingredients four times. Add milk very slowly while hot, mix well, add vanilla flavoring, put in whites of eggs, beaten till light. Bake 45 minutes in slow oven.

White Icing.

1½ cup powdered sugar; 2 tablespoons hot milk; ½ teaspoon butter; ½ teaspoon vanilla extract.

Add butter to hot milk, add sugar slowly to make right consistency to spread, then add vanilla. Spread on top and sides of cake.

Sunshine Cake.

3 tablespoons shortening, ¾ cup sugar, yolks of 3 eggs, 1 teaspoon flavoring extract, ½ cup milk, 1½ cups flour, 3 teaspoons baking powder. — Cover with white icing, same as used for above Angels Food.

MRS. DINA PRIESS.

Extra Hints for Baking.

1st quarter hour: Cake should rise but not brown.

2nd quarter hour: Continue to rise and specks of brown appear.

3rd quarter hour: Cake should brown evenly all over.

4th quarter hour: Cake should shrink from sides of pan.

Layer cakes bake in from 20 to 25 minutes.

Loaf cakes bake in from 40 to 60 minutes.

If cake sticks, lay a wet cloth over bottom of pan.

MISS META DIETZ.

Weights and Measures.

1 cup, medium size, ½ pint or ¼ lb.
4 cups, medium size, of flour weigh 1 lb.
1 pt. flour weighs ½ lb.
1 pt. white sugar weighs 1 lb.
2 tablespoonfuls of liquid weigh 1 oz.
8 teaspoonfuls of liquid weigh 1 oz.
1 gill of liquid weighs 4 oz.
1 pt. of liquid weighs 16 oz.

Sandwiches.

Chicken Sandwiches.

To a cupful of cold boiled chopped chicken, add a half cupful of almonds or pecans, one-fourth cupful of stuffed olives, also chopped fine, and enough mayonnaise dressing, to make of the right consistency. Spread thin slices of bread with butter, and place crisp lettuce leaves on these. Place the chicken filling between, and form into sandwiches.

MRS. R. G. STRIEGLER.

Egg Sandwiches.

Mince hard boiled eggs, mix with chopped olives, or cress and parsley, moisten with butter or mayonnaise. Salt, pepper to suit the taste. Spread between sliced bread.

MISS ALMA SCHUCH.

Pimento and Cheese Sandwiches.

1 cup grated cream cheese; 4 tablespoonfuls milk; 1 small can pimentoes; 2 tablespoonfuls butter; 1 teaspoonful salt; 1 teaspoonful cornstarch; paprika to taste.

Put cheese in double boiler, add salt, butter, paprika and cornstarch, dissolved in milk. Cook and stir until smooth. Remove from fire and add chopped pimento.

LETTIE RICHTER.

Ham Sandwiches.

1 cup boiled ham; ½ cup of chopped celery; 1 tablespoonful of chopped pickles; salad dressing.

Mince well some boiled ham. To every cupful of ham use a heaping tablespoonful of chopped pickles, and ½ cupful of chopped celery. Mix to a paste with salad dressing, and spread between slices of bread.

DRESSING: Beaten yolks of 4 eggs; ½ cup of sugar; 1 tablespoonful of salt; 1 teaspoonful of mustard; ½ teaspoonful of pepper; 1 teaspoonful of flour; ¾ pint of vinegar and a spoonful of butter.

Stir vinegar into the egg mixture slowly, to prevent curdling. Set in a cool place and when ready to use, thin with thick cream.

MRS. OTTO KOLMEIER.

Sardine Sandwiches.

1 can of sardines; hard boiled eggs; salt and pepper; lemon juice; melted butter.

Mash the sardines to a paste using all the oil in the can. Combine with an equal quantity of the mashed yolks of the eggs; add the chopped whites. Season with salt, pepper, and lemon juice and moisten with melted butter.

MRS. AUG. ITZ.

Salad Sandwiches.

Equal parts of cold boiled tongue and breast of chicken, chopped very fine and pounded to a paste; season with salt, celery salt, cayenne, or paprika, and moisten with mayonnaise or boiled dressing.

MRS. MAX BIERSCHWALE.

Delicious Sandwiches.

1 cup of ground ham; a few olives; 1 tablespoon of pickles; 1 tablespoon of pimentos; 3 tablespoons of mayonnaise dressing.

Spread the mixture on a crisp lettuce leaf between lightly buttered slices of white bread.

MRS. R. L. KOTT.

Tongue Sandwiches.

1 cupful of cold boiled tongue (mince fine); ½ cup celery; 1 large ripe tomato; 1 green sweet pepper; 2 or 3 small pickles, if desired.

Cut celery, tomatoes, pepper and pickles in small pieces and mix with tongue. Mix all with mayonnaise dressing.

ELSA WALTER.

Pecan Nut Sandwiches.

Rub to a smooth paste one teaspoon of butter, two tablespoonfuls of grated cheese, a saltspoonful each of salt, paprika, dry mustard and celery salt, a little anchovy paste and one teaspoonful of vinegar. When very smooth add one cupful of pecan nuts that have been passed through the meat chopper.

VERDIE KETTNER.

Tomato Sandwiches.

Peel some ripe tomatoes, remove the seeds, press out the water, season the pulp with pepper, salt, oil, vinegar and lastly a little freshly grated cheese.

VERDIE KETTNER.

Confectionery.

Hard Caramels.

One cup white sugar; one cup molasses; two squares chocolate; butter, size of a walnut.

Boil until brittle, when tested; then add one cup chopped nuts and pour on buttered pans.

MRS. LOUIS STIELER.

Chocolate Caramels.

2 cups molasses; 1 cup brown sugar; 1 cup cream or milk; ½ ℔ chocolate; butter, size of an egg.

Beat all together and boil until it thickens, when tested in cold water. Turn into large flat tins, well buttered. When nearly cold, cut into small squares.

MRS. ED. OEHLER.

Stuffed Dates.

1 ℔ dates (stoned, stuffed with pecans); fresh cocoanut (grated); make stiff white icing, roll dates in icing and then in cocoanut.

Stuffed Figs.

Stuff figs with nuts, soak over night in brandy, roll in powdered sugar.

MRS. RANDALL,
Sherman, Texas.

Date Roll.

1 ℔ dates; ½ cup milk; 2 cups sugar; 2 cups nuts.

Stone and chop dates, boil sugar and milk about 3 minutes, add dates and stir until dissolved, take off fire and beat until it begins to thicken, add nuts, beat again, roll into a wet cloth, and when cool, slice.

MISS BEULAH TALLEY.

Sweet Divinity.

In a saucepan put 2/3 cup water, 3 cups granulated sugar, and one cup Karo Corn Syrup. Let cook until the mixture will make a soft ball when tested in cold water.

Twelve minutes after first saucepan has been started, into a second one put ½ cup water and 1 cup granulated sugar, and set to cook. When this mixture threads, when dropped from a spoon, it is done. This will be very nearly the same time as the first is in proper condition. When the first is ready, the mixture should be poured slowly over the whites of 3 eggs whisked to a stiff froth, beating briskly the whites. When it has reached a satisfactory stage, turn in slowly the contents of the second saucepan, still beating constantly, and stir in a cup of nutmeats. Turn the mass out in a buttered tin and score in squares when sufficiently cool.

MISS E. LOUDON.
MRS. ALFRED SCHMIDT.

Divinity Candy.

2 2/3 cups sugar; 2/3 cup corn syrup; 2/3 cup water; whites of 2 eggs.

Cook sugar, syrup and water until it forms hard balls, when dropped into cold water. Have the whites of 2 eggs, beaten stiff, in a vessel large enough to hold all the candy. Pour candy over eggs slowly, beating hard all the time, and continue beating till almost hard. Then turn into a buttered dish to chalk. Cut into squares when cold. You may add any kind of nuts or raisins, before turning candy into buttered dish.

MRS. OTTO KOLMEIER.

Fig Fudge.

Two pounds light brown sugar; cover with rich sweet milk, one large tablespoonful butter. Cook until it will gum in cold water. Add a package of figs, chopped; flavor with vanilla; beat until stiff and pour on buttered plates.

MRS. LOUIS STIELER.

Genesee Squares.

2 cups sugar; 1 cup molasses; ½ cup butter; 1 cup milk; 2 cakes good sweet chocolate; 2 teaspoonfuls vanilla.

Grate chocolate and let the mixture come slowly to a boil. Let it boil until it will form a ball in cold water. Remove from fire, add vanilla and stir until it is thick and shows signs of sugaring. Spread in tins and cut into cubes.

MISS ELSBETH HANISCH.

Molasses Fudge.

3 cups of granulated sugar; 1 cup of milk or cream; 1 tablespoonful of butter; 2 tablespoonfuls of molasses; ½ teaspoonful of soda, dissolved in a little milk.

Boil 10 minutes. Beat until creamy; add 1 teaspoonful of vanilla and 1 cup of nut meats while beating. When cold cut into squares.

MRS. A. H. WELGEHAUSEN.

Candy Patience.

2 cups sugar; ½ cup sweet milk; 1 teaspoon vanilla.

Put 1½ cups sugar in sauce pan and melt. Cook the remainder with the milk until it hardens when put in water. Add the melted sugar and stir five minutes. Put in buttered dish and cut in squares.

MISS MAYME GREATHOUSE.

Marshmallows.

Boil 2 cups of sugar; ½ cup of water; till it forms a syrup. Dissolve one envelope of Knox Gelatine in ½ cup of water and let it stand 5 minutes. Pour boiling syrup over dissolved gelatine and beat till stiff.

Then, pour half of portion into a buttered pan, to the other half add pink coloring which comes in gelatine. Use any flavor desired, making each half different. Let it stand until it is hard enough to be cut into blocks.

RUBY STEIN.

Nut Candy.

2 cups sugar; ½ cup water; 1 cup nutmeats.

Boil sugar and water without stirring until thick enough to spin a thread; flavor to suit taste; set in cold water; stir quickly until white, then stir in the nuts; turn into flat tins; when cold cut into squares.

MISS E. LOUDON.

Wellesley Pinoche.

2 cups light brown sugar; 1 cup milk; butter, size of an egg; 1 cup chopped nuts.

Boil sugar, butter and milk together until mixture thickens when tested in cold water; add nuts, beat until a thick and creamy mass; pour out into well-buttered pan, before it has quite cooled. Cut into squares with a knife that has been dipped in boiling water.

ESTELLE F. SMITH.

Taffy.

3 cups sugar; ½ cup water; ½ cup of vinegar; butter, size of an egg; vanilla.

Mix all together, cook until it hardens when dropped in cold water. Don't stir, turn on greased platter and pull until white.

MRS. LOUIS STIELER.

French Nougat.

2 whites of eggs, beaten stiffly; 2½ cups sugar; ½ cup warm water; ½ cup corn syrup; 1½ cups nuts, candied cherries, raisins and citron, mixed.

Boil sugar, syrup and water until it threads, pour half the quantity slowly into the well beaten whites of eggs, whipping incessantly. Allow the remainder to boil until it forms a hard glassy ball when dropped into water, and add the other which in the meantime has been steadily beaten. When almost hard, add fruit. Drop on oiled paper and wrap when cooled.

MRS. WILLIE PETERMANN.

After Dinner Mints.

2 cups granulated sugar; ¾ cups of water (cold or warm); 1/8 teaspoonful cream of tartar.

Stir the mixture well before placing on stove; do not stir when boiling. Boil until when dropped in cold water it will roll in a soft ball between the fingers. When done, pour into buttered dish and allow it to become almost cool. Add a small drop of oil of peppermint and beat until of a creamy consistency. Work with the hands until plastic; mould with fingers into the shape desired and place moulded fondant on oiled paper.

The fondant may be flavored with vanilla, lemon, or strawberry and mixed with chopped raisins, dates, cocoanut, pecans, or walnuts, then moulded into fancy shapes.

JULIA ESTILL.

Fruit Fudge.

3 cups of sugar, ¼ cup of cocoanut, 1 cup of nuts, ¼ cup of figs, ¼ cup of dates, ¼ cup of raisins, ¾ cup of milk, 3 teaspoonfuls cocoa, butter the size of an egg.

Boil sugar, butter and milk till it forms a soft ball when tested in cold water, then add the fruit, mix well and turn in buttered dish. When nearly cold cut into squares.

MRS. HUGO KLIER.

Nut Candy.

2½ cups of sugar. butter the size of an egg, 3 tablespoonfuls of vinegar. Melt butter, add sugar and vinegar. Boil until brown, stirring continually. Lastly add, one cup of nut meats, pour on buttered dish and cut into squares.

MRS. HUGO KLIER.

Jellies and Preserves.

Fruit Jellies.

With but a **few exceptions**, the rule for all fruit jellies is substantially the same. The **directions given**, if followed closely, cannot fail to produce a clear, sparkling jelly. If it should, after strict adherence to the recipe, **prove watery**, the fault is in the fruit, not in the method or the maker.

Thin liquid jellies can often be brought to greater firmness if the filled glasses are allowed to stand in the hot sun. Sometimes three or four hours will suffice, at other times as many days may be required.

Not until the jelly is at least comparatively firm should it be covered with waxed paper and sealed.

MRS. OTTO KOLMEIER.

Melon Preserve.

1 ℔ melon; 1 ℔ sugar; rind of 1 lemon.

Peel the melon and scrape out the red flesh, using only the hard part, cut into pieces and cover with vinegar for 24 hours. Then drain and cover melon with the sugar for the same length of time. Take out and let sugar come to a boil, then add the melon and lemon rind. Boil until partly soft, take out melon and boil juice until thick enough. Let cool and fill into jars.

MRS. FRED WALTER.

Crab Apple Jelly.

Quarter, without peeling or coring, ripe crab apples. Put into preserving kettle, add water, not quite enough to cover the fruit, boil slowly until fruit is quite tender.

Strain through a flannel bag. Measure juice. To each pint of this, allow a pound of sugar. Place the juice on the stove, bring rapidly to a boil. Boil 20 minutes, skim it, add the sugar, stir until it has dissolved. Boil about 10 minutes longer. Test by cooling a little in a saucer.

Blackberries, Mustang Grapes, Plums, etc., can all be made by following the above recipe.

MRS. OTTO KOLMEIER.

Peach Jelly.

Select peaches that are not too sweet. Wash them and rub off the fuzz. Cut in halves; remove the stones. Crack a dozen kernels, and add them to the peaches. Boil until tender. When the liquid is strained and measured, add a tablespoonful of lemon juice to each pint of the jelly, and then proceed as in other jellies.

MRS. WM. CRENWELGE.

Fig Preserves.

4 ℔ of peeled figs; 3 ℔ of sugar; one lemon.

Peel figs in the evening and cover with sugar. Next morning add the lemon juice, or sliced lemon, and cook about 2½ hours, or until the fruit looks transparent, and the syrup is like honey.

MRS. R. G. STRIEGLER.

Orange Marmalade.

The rind and juice of three oranges, shredded finely; ¾ quart of water.

Soak for 24 hours. Add 1¼ qts. of sugar to every quart of the mixture and boil until it has the color and consistency of honey.   MISS BERTHA OCHS.

Peach Marmalade.

To each pound of peeled and stoned peaches, cut in halves, allow three-quarters of a pound of sugar. Put sugar in your preserving kettle, add water to dissolve, let come to a boil. Add your peaches which should be good and firm so as not to cook to pieces. Boil carefully for about half an hour, lift out of the juice and arrange on platters and set in the hot sun to partly dry and toughen.

Turn them occasionally. The next day heat the syrup to boiling, drop in the peaches, also about a dozen kernels of the peach-stones, chopped fine, and the juice of a lemon. Cook until the peaches are clear and the marmalade is jelly-like. Test it by cooling a little in a saucer.

Pear Marmalade may be made by the same recipe.
   MRS. OTTO KOLMEIER.

Pie Melon Preserves.

Slice a pie melon in lengthwise strips, each about two inches long. Cover with equal parts of vinegar and water. Let them remain until the next day. Drain them. Then cook with equal parts of melon and sugar, and one lemon rind.   MRS. AUG. ITZ.

Pie Melon Preserves.

Cover 8 ℔ of finely cut melon pulp with 4 lb of sugar. Leave standing over night, then add 4 sliced lemons, and cook several hours.
   MRS. HERMAN HOHENBERGER.

CATSUP, PICKLES, CANNED VEGETABLES, ETC.

Hints on Canning.

What is canning? Canning is the art of preserving food by means of sterilization by heat, and keeping it sterile in an air-tight, sealed container.

The most troublesome foes to combat in canning, are the bacteria.

Never use commercial preservatives or canning powders, as they are dangerous. Use heat.

Do your canning by the "Cold Pack Method", because in this way the bacteria have no chance.

Save all of your fruits and vegetables you raise, and store them in the cellar, as canned goods. This does the cooking for the whole year in a few days, and that's one time you can get the old man to help you cook if you get him to help you can.

Last but not least, "Can while you can, so you can have a can, when there is nothing to can.

ALFRED NEFFENDORF.

Chili Sauce.

6 doz. tomatoes; 12 cups vinegar; 2 dozen onions; 24 tablespoons sugar; 12 teaspoons ginger; 12 teaspoons cloves; 12 teaspoons cinnamon; 12 teaspoons salt.

Red pepper to suit taste.

Boil 4 or 5 hours, or down to about half of original quantity.

MRS. AD. WEHMEYER.

Chili Sauce.

12 large ripe tomatoes; 2 cupfuls sugar; 1 large onion; 1 tablespoonful salt; 4 red peppers; 1 tablespoonful vinegar; 1 tablespoonful each of ground allspice and cloves.

Chop fine the tomatoes, onions and peppers. Add the other ingredients and boil until quite thick.

MRS. HUGO BASSE.

Pepper Hash.

Remove the seeds and chop very fine 12 sweet red peppers, and 12 green peppers and 12 very small onions. Add 3 tablespoonfuls of salt and allow the mixture to simmer for 10 minutes. Then drain, and add 1 quart of diluted vinegar and 1 cupful of sugar. Add a little mustard and celery seed, if liked. Let the hash come to a boil, then pour it into jars and seal while hot.

MRS. HERMANN HOHENBERGER.
MRS. DINA PRIESS.

Cucumber Pickles.

Take one gallon of diluted vinegar, and one cup each of dry mustard and salt, or if sweet pickles are wanted add one or two cups of sugar. Pick your cucumbers in the morning, wash them thoroughly and drain, then drop them into the vinegar.

MRS. A. H. KNEESE.

Ripe Cucumbers.

Peel cucumbers, and cut into eight parts, hollow out seeds and pulps with a silver spoon. To a bucket of cucumbers use 1 cup salt. Salt pieces well and allow them to stand 24 hours. Wipe dry with clean cloth.

Cook vinegar thinned with water to taste; to 1 quart vinegar use 1 tablespoonful of sugar, 2 bay leaves and a handful of mustard seed.

Pack in fruit jars, pour boiling vinegar over all and seal tight.

ROSA DECHERT.

Salt Cucumber Pickles.

Wash cucumbers with a brush, put into cold water over night. Drain them the next morning and pack closely into jar, one layer cucumbers, then a layer grape leaves and grapes, and so on till jar is filled.

To two quarts of water add one cup of salt, fill the jar with the salt and water, cover up, with a light weight on top to keep pickles under water.

MRS. JACOB GOLD, SR.

Chow Chow.

Beans, cabbage, tomatoes, onions.

To every gallon of cut vegetables add: 1 tablespoonful of salt; 1 tablespoonful of pepper; 1½ tablespoonfuls of mustard; 2 tablespoonfuls of molasses; ½ teaspoonful of cloves; 1 quart of vinegar.

Boil half an hour.

MRS. JUL. KLINGELHOEFER.

Cucumber Pickles.

Take green cucumbers, about 4 or 5 inches long, soak 48 hours in strong brine, then pour off the brine and rinse with cold water.

Boil together 1 quart of vinegar and ½ quart of water. Fill jars with the cucumbers, add to a two quart jar 4 small red peppers, ½ teaspoon whole black peppers, a piece of alum the size of a small teaspoon, to restore the green color of cucumbers, pour the boiling vinegar over and seal tight.

ANNA GOLD.

Dill Pickles.

Wash medium sized cucumbers, cover with cold water and allow to remain over night. Drain them the next day, wipe dry, and pack closely together in stone jars using plenty of fresh dill between the layers of cucumbers. To each half-gallon jar add 2 small red peppers, 1 teaspoonful of black peppers, and 2 bay leaves. To 6 quarts of water add 1 lb of rock salt and a small teaspoonful of alum. Heat the mixture to the boiling point, add 1 quart of pure cider vinegar and pour at once over the pickles covering them well. Seal tightly, while hot. If fresh dill cannot be obtained, use dill seed in the proportion of a tablespoonful to each half-gallon jar. Fresh dill gives a better flavor to the pickles.

MRS. OTTO KOLMEIER.

Chow Chow.

Chop fine tomatoes, sweet peppers, and onions. Salt over night, (each separately). Next morning wash the vegetables and drain through a cheese cloth. When drained put into jars. Boil vinegar and red peppers, pour over and seal tightly.

MRS. H. CORDES.

Sweet Pickle Cucumbers.

Cucumbers; 3 quarts of vinegar; 1 cup of water; 2 cups of sugar; black pepper, green grapes and a branch of dill.

Wash well one bucket of medium sized cucumbers, place in brine that will float an egg and let stand over night. In the morning wash cucumbers in fresh water and wipe dry. Let the sugar, vinegar and water come to a boil, add cucumbers and boil for ten minutes. Press the cucumbers in a glass jar, with a little whole black pepper, a small bunch of green grapes and a little branch of dill. Fill with the boiling vinegar and seal.

MRS. F. STEIN.

Dill Pickles.

1 gal. small cucumbers; 2 qts. water; 2/3 qts. vinegar; 1/3 qt. salt; 4 tablespoonfuls dill seed; 2 tablespoonfuls allspice and hot pepper; grape leaves and a small piece of alum.

Lay the cucumbers in cold water over night. In the morning put them in jars in layers with grape leaves and spices. Let salt, vinegar and water come to a boil and pour hot over cucumbers.

MRS. LOUIS OEHLER.

Piccalilli.

8 quarts green tomatoes, chopped fine; 1 quart onions, chopped fine; 1 quart green peppers, chopped fine. Mix with ¾ cup of salt and let stand over night.

Then squeeze very dry, put in a kettle, cover with good vinegar and bring to a boil. Add 2 dozen cloves, 1 dozen allspice, 2 oz. mustard, ¼ teaspoons cayenne and 2 cups sugar, and cook about one hour.

Put up and seal air-tight.

MISS ANNA GOLD.

Stuffed Peppers (Sweet).

Core the peppers, sprinkle with salt, pour over with boiling water, and stand over night. Then cut up cabbage, boil in salt water not too soft, squeeze the juice from the cabbage and put cabbage in peppers; make a sauce of 1 cup of vinegar, 2 cups of water, 3 tablespoonfuls of sugar, a few pickle spices, let come to a boil, put in peppers and boil for a few minutes, put in jar and seal up tightly.

MRS. H. CORDES.

Stuffed Pickled Peppers.

2 doz. green peppers; 1 small head of white cabbage; 4 large white onions; 3 tablespoonfuls mustard seed; ½ teaspoonful powdered cloves; ½ teaspoonful powdered allspice; 2 teaspoonfuls salt.

Remove the stem ends of the peppers, take out all the seeds and place in strong salt water for 48 hours. After 48 hours remove from salt water and dry well.

Chop the vegetables fine and mix well; fill peppers and replace the stem ends and tie with white thread; put in a stone jar and fill with boiled vinegar. After twenty-four hours boil the vinegar again and pour over peppers and repeat in another twenty-four hours. Cover the jar and put in a dark place.

MRS. ALVIN STRIEGLER.

Mixed Pickles.

1 qt. small cucumbers; 1 qt. onions; 1 qt. sliced green tomatoes; 1 qt. cauliflower, cut into small pieces; 2 qts. vinegar; 3 cups sugar; 8 tablespoonfuls mustard; ½ cup flour; 1 teaspoonful turmeric; 1 teaspoonful cayenne pepper.

Sprinkle the vegetables with salt and let stand over night. Put the vinegar in a porcelain kettle and when boiling, add the well mixed dry ingredients, and then the vegetables, which previously must have been boiled about ten minutes in weak vinegar.

MRS. BANNOWSKY.

Sweet Mixed Pickles.

4 tablespoons mustard seed; 2 tablespoons ginger; 4 tablespoons celery seed; 1 tablespoon ground mustard; 1 tablespoon mace; 1 tablespoon turmeric; 1 tablespoon cinnamon bark; 1 qt. sugar.

Soak vegetables over night in brine strong enough to carry an egg. Boil vinegar, sugar, and spices about 5 minutes, then put in well drained vegetables, let simmer for about 5 minutes, put in jars, and seal while hot. This is enough for one peck of pickles.

MRS. AD. WEHMEYER.

Sweet Mixed Pickles.

Small head of cauliflower; 1 qt. small carrots; small head of cabbage; 1 qt. of beans; one or two quarts of small white onions; 1 qt. of small cucumbers; spices and vinegar sauce.

Peel onions the day before and cover with salt over night. Cook each kind of vegetable in separate salt water for five or ten minutes, with the exception of the cucumbers. The cucumbers should not be over two inches long, and after washing, are also covered with salt over night, and are not cooked, only drained from the brine next day.

Mix all the vegetables, and fill into glass jars, covering them with the following vinegar sauce:

To 3 pints of vinegar take 2 pints of water, one ℔ of sugar, a little allspice, mustard seed, a few small red peppers, whole black peppers, and any other spices you may like. Let this come to boiling point and pour at once over the pickles, covering them well. Seal while hot.

MRS. WM. WEYRICH.

Tomato Catsup.

2 tablespoonfuls of salt; 3 tablespoonfuls of sugar; ½ gallon of vinegar; 1 gallon of tomato juice; 1 teaspoon of black pepper; 1 teaspoon of red pepper; 1 teaspoonful of mustard.

Let all boil 1 hour, then bottle while hot, and seal.

MRS. G. E. WRIGHT.

Tomato Catsup.

1 gal. tomatoes (strained); 6 tablespoonfuls of salt; 3 tablespoonfuls of black pepper; 1 tablespoonful of cloves; 2 tablespoonfuls of cinnamon; 2 tablespoonfuls of allspice; 1½ pints of vinegar.

Boil down to one-half original quantity.

MRS. HUGO BASSE.

Tomato Catsup.

1 bucket ripe tomatoes; 3 large onions; 2 small pieces garlic. Chop onions and garlic in small pieces, tie in a cloth and boil with tomatoes until well done. Then strain. Tie 1 tablespoon allspice; 1 tablespoon cloves; 1 tablespoon black pepper in a cloth and boil with pulp 1 teaspoon cayenne pepper; 3 tablespoons salt; ¾ quart vinegar, boil 3 hours.

MRS. MAX T. HENKE.

Sweet Pickled Peaches and Plums.

8 ℔ fruit; 1 qt. vinegar; 4 ℔ sugar; 2 oz. whole cinnamon; 2 oz. cloves.

Preferably take clingstone peaches, either peel or rub off down with coarse towel. Boil sugar, vinegar and spices 5 minutes, put in peaches, a few at a time, with a clove inserted into each. When done, test by pricking with a fork, remove, place in jars and use liquid for remaining fruit. When fruit are all in jars, simmer down the liquid to the desired consistency (about half the original quantity), pour over fruit and seal while very hot.

MRS. LOUIS OEHLER.
MISS ANNA GOLD.
MRS. C. W. FEUGE.

Green Tomato Pickle.

Cut up 1 peck of green tomatoes, sprinkle with salt and let stand 24 hours. Strain off liquid, mix tomatoes with 1 teaspoonful each of black pepper, cloves, nutmeg, cinnamon; 12 small red peppers; 3 onions; 1 cup brown sugar.

Cover with vinegar and boil for 3 hours.

Put in jars and seal at once.

MISS IRMA OCHS.

Sweet Peach Pickle.

10 ℔ of peaches; 4 ℔ of sugar; 1 qt. of good vinegar; whole black peppers; 2 oz. of stick cinnamon; 1 oz. of whole cloves.

Select small, firm peaches. Dip them in boiling water, then wipe dry. Boil together for five minutes the sugar, vinegar, and spices. Then put in one layer of peaches and let boil from three to five minutes; take out and put in a jar. Add peaches again until all are used. Fill each jar with the syrup and seal.

MRS. R. L. KOTT.
MRS. HENRY BASSE.

Canned Beans.

String and slice beans, boil in a little salt water until tender, drain and cool.

Boil ½ cup water; ½ cup vinegar; 1 tablespoonful sugar. When cold, pour over beans in jars and seal, taking care not to fill the jars too closely.

MRS. GEO. E. WRIGHT.

Mustard Beans.

1 gal. sliced beans; 1 gal. sliced onions; 1 quart water; ¼ quart vinegar; 2 cups sugar; ½ cup salt; 2 tablespoons black pepper; 8 tablespoons mustard.

Mix all thoroughly and cook 1 hour. Seal while hot.

MRS. ALFRED GROBE.

Canned Beans.

Boil in salt water, put into jars, adding one tablespoonful of vinegar and one of sugar to each quart jar. Fill jar with freshly boiling water, and seal at once.

Canned Corn.

12 cups of corn; 1 cup of sugar; ¾ cup of salt; 1 cup of water.

Boil five minutes, pour into jars while hot.

MRS. WM. CRENWELGE.

Canned Corn.

8 pints corn; 3 pints salt. Add a little water to the corn, cook for 20 minutes, then add the salt and cook 5 minutes longer. Put in jars while hot.

MRS. ALFRED SCHMIDT.

Corn Relish.

10 cups corn, cut from cob; 10 cups cabbage, chopped fine; 5 large sweet red peppers, chopped fine; ½ quart vinegar, white; 3 tablespoons salt; 2 cups sugar; 4 tablespoons white mustard seed; 2 tablespoons celery seed.

Mix thoroughly and cook half hour.

MRS. MAX BIERSCHWALE.

Sweet Pickle Cabbage.

Pick cabbage and grind fine, put on stove, cover in clear water. Add little salt. Cook until tender. When done drain all water off in a vessel, then add 1 cup of that water that the cabbage was cooked in. Add to that 1 cup sugar, 1 cup good vinegar, let cook 20 minutes, then put in jar and seal while hot.

MRS. ED. WINKEL.

For
Service
Comfort
And
Courtesy
Yours

TRAVELERS HOTEL
Nagel & Wuest
SAN ANTONIO, TEXAS
U. S. A.

OLD STAND MEAT MARKET

Main St., Fredericksburg, Texas.

Richard Henke, Proprietor.

Fresh Beef, Pork, Mutton, Lard, Ham and Sausage always on hand.

The Loan and Abstract Co.

R. G. Striegler, Manager.

ABSTRACTS, LOANS, FIRE INSURANCE.

A. P. C. Petsch, Attorney. E. C. Hansen, Real Estate.

G. A. Duerler Mfg. Co.
San Antonio, Texas

Wolesale Candy Manufacturers

Oldest Candy Factory in the State

Keidel & Kallenberg

Handle the best and completest line of goods to be had for the sick-room as well as for the kitchen. If your family is sick ring 25 or if you need some drug in the kitchen do the same. Try some of Our Baking Powder. It's made here.

Our Motto: Money Refunded If Not Satisfactory..

MAX T. HENKE
Fredericksburg, Texas

Staple and Fancy Groceries;

Poultry, Butter, Eggs, Country Produce.

Free Delivery   Phone No. 302.

"SKY HIGH"

The Flour that insures you good Bread, Cakes, Rolls, and Pastry

TRY A SACK, SOLD BY

GOLD & STAHL

Free Delivery   Phone 97

Schandua & Reichenau
Tinners
Fredericksburg, Texas.

THE VOGUE
Fredericksburg, Texas.

We Specialize on all Women's Apparel. Fine Millinery, Ready to Wear, Dress Goods, Trimmings, and Notions.

PHONE 56.   **THE HOUSE OF QUALITY.**

CORNER CONFECTIONERY

Makers of Pure Velvet Ice Cream. Sold in any quantity. Send us your orders. Special orders for parties, picnics, etc. We serve only the best at our Fountain.

WALTER C. KLAERNER, Proprietor
Fredericksburg, Texas.

SCHMIDT BROS.
Dealers in
Dry Goods, Notions, Glassware, Hardware, Crockery.

We handle the celebrated "Brown Shoe" makers of Buster Browns, Maxine, White House, Blue Ribbon. We buy and sell for cash only.

SADDLES AND HARNESS, SADDLERY, HARDWARE.

OTTO EVERS

Local Agent for
STEWART SHEARING MACHINES.
Fredericksburg, Texas.
Shoe Repairing in Connection.

Food economy now, more than ever, demands the purchase and use of those food articles of known high quality and absolute purity and healthfulness.

ROYAL

Is a Pure, Cream of Tartar
BAKING POWDER
Contains No Alum

Perfectly leavens and makes the food more delicious and wholesome.

The Favorite of Fredericksburg.

House Wives and Millions of others—as well as Domestic Science Teachers everywhere.

Calumet Baking Powder

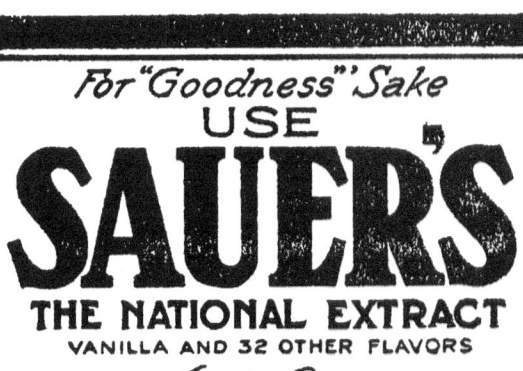

Cuts Waste and Saves Time

Economical and careful housewives everywhere are finding new baking joys by the use of

Miss PRINCINE

Pure Phosphate Baking Powder

This is the new-fashioned baking powder which requires heat to develop its full leavening strength. MISS PRINCINE is also the choice of food experts at many of the big food shows in the East.

Bakings of delicious taste and feathery lightness are your sure reward if you use MISS PRINCINE—the baking powder that rises as it bakes and bakes as it rises.

In the randy-handled cups:

1 ℔ net weight 35c   ½ ℔ net weight 20c

11 ounce can, 25c

In the handy-handled pails:

2½ ℔ 75c   5 ℔ $1.50

OTTO KOLMEIER
HARDWARE, TINWARE, ROOFING

Guttering, Ranges, Cooking and Heating Stoves, Guns and Ammunition, Fishing Tackle, Washing Machines, Separators, Refrigerators, all kinds of Wire, Galvanized Tanks.

SAGEBIEL MILLINERY COMPANY

We make a specialty of a select and stylish assortment of **MILLINERY, HATS FOR LADIES, MISSES, AND CHILDREN**, Trimmings, etc., at reasonable prices. Your visit to our store will be highly appreciated.

F. H. Petermann & Co.
"Butchers"

Fresh Meats, Sausage, Ham, Lard and Bacon.

Prompt Delivery　　　　　　　　　　　　　　　　Phone 77

Fredericksburg, Texas.

FRANK HANISCH
Druggist

Fredericksburg, Texas.　　　　　　　　　　　　Phone 169.

We stock all worthy remedies as well as toilet pre-

GARAGE
LOUIS KOTT & CO.

Authorized Ford Sales and Service

Fredericksburg, Texas.

G. H. Houy & Son

Dealers In

Furniture. Undertakers and Embalmers.

FREDERICKSBURG,   TEXAS.

H. Kuenemann

Fredericksburg, Texas.

Lumber, Hardware, Paints, And Oil.

PHONE NO. 31

OSTROW HOTEL

We Carry In Stock

the simple and easy-running

Deering Binders, J. I. Case Threshing Machines, Moline and Canton (single and double) Riding Planters and Cultivaters, Bain Wagons, Hay Rakes, Grass Mowers, Hay Presses, Moline Universal Tractors. All products of the best factories kept in Stock. Come and see us if in need of anything in our line.

CARTER & WEIRICH
Fredericksburg, Texas.

COLLINS COMPANY
Wholesale Grocers and Importers

San Antonio, Fredericksburg, Kerrville, and Uvalde, Texas

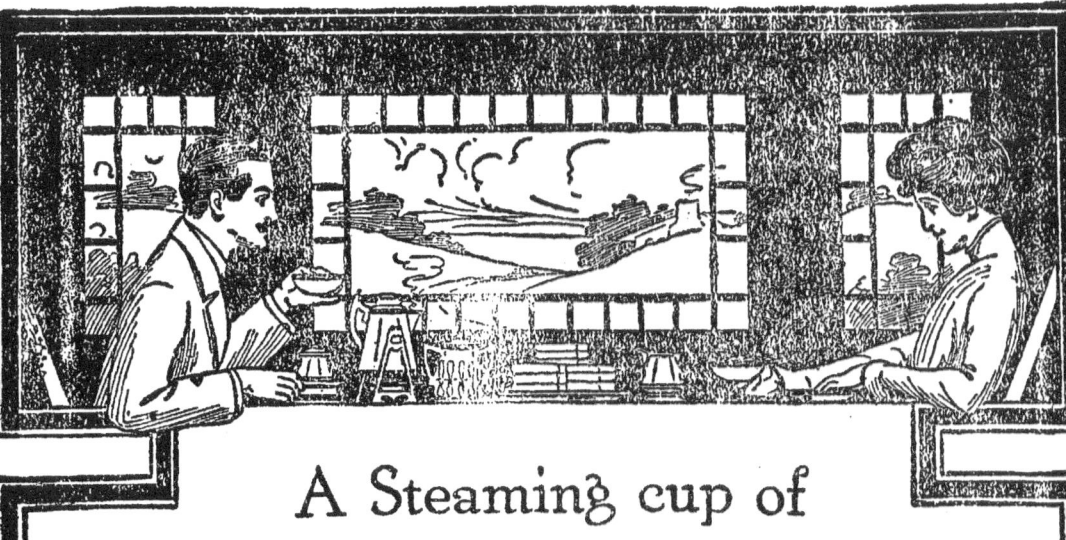

A Steaming cup of

Maxwell House Coffee

at meal time whets the appetite and fills the mind with anticipations of real enjoyment.

Guaranteed absolutely pure and the finest obtainable.

Sealed Cans at Grocers

CHEEK-NEAL COFFEE CO.,
NASHVILLE   HOUSTON   JACKSONVILLE

UP TOWN MEAT MARKET
HENKE BROS.
Main St., Fredericksburg, Tex.

Fresh Beef, Mutton, Sausage, Lard
Ham and Bacon always on hand.

Prompt Delivery   Phone No. 4:

JUENKE & SCHOENEWOLF
DEALERS IN
GENERAL MERCHANDISE

Ladies' and Gents' Furnishing Goods, Dry Goods, Groceries, Shelf Hardware, All Country Produce

Alfred Grobe
Fruit Stand, Phone 227

Fruit, Candies, Fresh Vegetables, Cold Drinks, Agent Magnolia Oil and Gasoline

Dr. Felix Keidel   **KEIDEL BROS.**   Dr. Werner Keide
Dentists

Mouth-wash. A sure cure and gives instant relief. Made by Anti-Zyma Dental Medicine Co., Fredericksburg, Texas. Sold by all Druggists.

Arthur Schaetter

Headquarters for

THE CELEBRATED "PATHE" PHONOGRAPHS.

A large assortment of Records on hand. Also Agent for Hoffmann, Kimball, Gulbransen, Kohler & Kimball, Ivers & Ponds Pianos, Autopianos and Players. Sample Instruments in Stock. Come and try them.

CONVENIENCE AND SAFETY

are assured by patronizing one of the most important Home Industries in Fredericksburg

The Fredericksburg Light & Power Co.

in using Electric Lights, Power for your Electric Irons, Carpet Sweepers, Toasters, Stoves, and Washing Machines.

The Only One

of its kind in Fredericksburg!

A modern Machine Shop, equipped with Oxy-Acetylene Gas Apparatus for welding all kinds of metals. First Class Blacksmith-Shop in Connection.

"Auto Repairing"   "Brunswick Tires"

FELIX W. MAIER, Proprietor.

Its the quality of
LIBERTY BELL FLOUR
that insures better baking

LIBERTY MILLS

San Antonio, Texas.

Loyal Music Store
Fredericksburg, Texas.

An Exclusive Music Store

Headquarters for the Genuine Victrola and Victrola Records. Pianos and Player Pianos

---

GUS MALCHOW

New and Second-hand Furniture

Buy, Sell, Trade, Rent or Exchange

CITIZENS GARAGE

JOSEPH BROS., Proprietors.

Next to Bank of Fredericksburg.

"Home for the Dodge Cars". Repairing on all kinds of Automobiles promptly done.

Wilbur C. Treadwell
OPTOMETRIST

Specialist in examination of the Eyes and fitting of Glasses.

Room 1.   Gold Building.

Fredericksburg, Texas.

Miss Bertha Priess.   Mrs. H. W. Kusenberger.

THE PARISIAN
"Priess & Kusenberger"

Millinery, Fancy Dress Goods, Notions, Ladies Furnishings and Ready-to-Wear. Phone No. 314.

PATRONIZE HOME INDUSTRY
by using:
PURE CRYSTALLIZED ICE

ROSENBERG'S
GOLD MEDAL COFFEE

It's Strictly Pure.
Rich In Aroma - Delicious In Taste. Sold under an absolute guarantee, at

COCKRELL'S
The Store that cuts prices on everything.

WELGEHAUSENS
5, 10, 15, and 25c Goods

Kodak Finishing

A. H. Welgehausen - - - - - Sole Owner

STUCKE'S BAKERY AND CONFECTIONERY
The Place Of Sweets

Bread, Rolls and Cakes, Modern Baked, Wholesome and Appetizing.

Ice Cream, Candies and Soda Fountain in connection.

Boerne   Fredericksburg   Mason

THE LAW OFFICES OF

WEINHEIMER & CO.
General Merchandise

Carry a well selected Stock of Dry Goods, Clothing, Boots, Shoes, Hats, Staple and Fancy Groceries.

THE BEST OF EVERYTHING

Fredericksburg Bottling Works

JACOB KRAUS, Proprietor

All kinds of Soda Water

Specialties: Coca Cola and Orange Julep

Manufacturer of Fine Cigars

A SUMMARY

of the Recipes in this Book leaves the impression that care must be exercised in the selection of INGREDIENTS in the preparation of ALL GOOD things to eat, and that QUALITY is the WATCHWORD in securing these.

Henke & Hirsch

Consider Quality in preference to quantity in ALL their merchandise, and you may feel secure that you get the best of what is to be had when you buy at their store. No Schemes, No Baits, but you will find your money will buy just as much, or even more, there, and reliable goods, at that, as anywhere.

FREDERICKSBURG, TEXAS.

Star Brand Flour

> Success in cooking is bound to follow a proper application of tried recipes coupled with a careful selection of ingredients

The importance of choosing a GOOD FLOUR cannot be overestimated.

NEW WAY   **Watch for the Star**
    AMBROSIA
        GALVESTON BELLS
            TIDAL WAVE
                ANITA

Watch for the Star

Are guaranteed to give perfect satisfaction
Manufactured by

TEXAS STAR FLOUR MILLS
GALVESTON, TEXAS.

The largest Wheat and Corn Products factory in

FREDERICKSBURG PUBLISING CO.

Wm. Dietel, Manager & Editor.
Wm. Habenicht, Business Manager.
I. G. Wehmeyer, Technical Dept.

FREDERICKSBURG - - - - - - - - - - - - - - - TEXAS.

———O———

Wochenblatt
$2.00 per year

Standard
$1.50 per year

———O———

We do all kinds of job work, both English and German, promptly, neatly, and accurately. Estimates cheerfully furnished.

This Cook Book is a sample of our work, it was printed and bound in our shop.

(Unincorporated)

FREDERICKSBURG, TEXAS.

Oscar Krauskopf, President.
Mrs. Alf. Vander Stucken, Vice President.
Wm. Bierschwale, Cashier.
Max J. Bierschwale, Asst. Cashier.
Walter F. Bierschwale, Asst. Cashier.

YOUR ACCOUNTS SOLICITED.

Nagel Bros. Monumental Works.

Owners of Celebrated
BEAR MOUNTAIN RED GRANITE QUARRIES
One of the finest grained Granites in U. S.
Fredericksburg, Texas.

Ask your Grocer for:

HUGHES

X X WHITE OR PICKLING VINEGAR
Best for pickling and table use!

R. M. HUGHES & CO.

Louisville, Ky.,   San Antonio, Texas.

ED. KNOPP
TIN SHOP

Dealer in Stoves, Tin and Enambled Ware. Agent for the "White Lily" Washing Machines, New Perfection and Florence Oil Stoves.

Oscar Krauskopf
Dealer in

Farm Implements, Water Supply Material

The Auto Oil Aermotor Windmill. Sanitary Plumbing, Etc.

FARMERS PRODUCE CO.

Agents for

Landas Flour and all Mill Products

Use "Minnehaha" and "Perfection" Flour. The Flour without regrets on Baking Day.

ROBERT BLUM
GENERAL MERCHANDISE

Fredericksburg   Texas.

Call for "Pioneer" Flou, best on market. We buy Cotton, Wheat, Oats, and all Country Produce.

Store Phone No. 8   Warehouse Phone No. 238

Bank Of Fredericksburg

(Unincorporated)

Member American Bankers Assn.
Member Texas Bankers Assn.

ONE OF THE OLDEST AND STRONGEST BANKS IN THE WEST.

Stockholders:

Temple D. Smith	Adolph Gold
Albert Koennecke	Mrs. Fred Walter
	Elsa Walter

Your Money in this Bank is insured against all loss by Robbery or Fire.

Temple D. Smith, President.	Ad. Gold, Active Vice. Pres.
Alb. Koennecke, Cashier.	Alex W. Henke, Asst. Cashier.

Lawrence Knopp, Asst. Cashier.

Pioneer Flour Mills

"Pioneer Flour"

---Unbleached---

No Chemicals

Pioneer Flour Mills

SAN ANTONIO,   Since 1851

care of their clothes as they are about the cooking. That's the reason why many let us do their **cleaning** and pressing.

STEHLING BROS.

THE CENTRAL DRUG CO.

has the best for you in:

Biological Products, Drugs, Patent Medicines.

Columbia Grafonolas, Records, Toilet Articles, and Books

F. STEIN & SON

WHY NOT OWN YOUR OWN HOME?

Let F. Stein & Son help you plan your new home.

PHONE 230.

PHONE 268—A GROCERY NUMBER!

Use it often, for your Grocery Wants! We deliver promptly. We handle the best brands of Flour, Extracts and Spices.

QUALITY CASH GROCERY

W. E. Knoche.   Reuben Bernhardt.

u tivators, agons,
combined, Tractors and Engines, also Cream Separators.

First Class Garage in Connection.

ARTHUR KELLER

Headquarters for

FARMS, RANCHES, AND CITY PROPERTY.

"Loans made Promptly."

Office in Klaerner Bldg.   Phone 275.

Fredericksburg, Texas.

You Can Bake Bread Perfectly With This Oil Stove

If you think it is impossible to bake bread or pastries on an oil stove, come in and see the new-tipe, all the year' round, wickless.

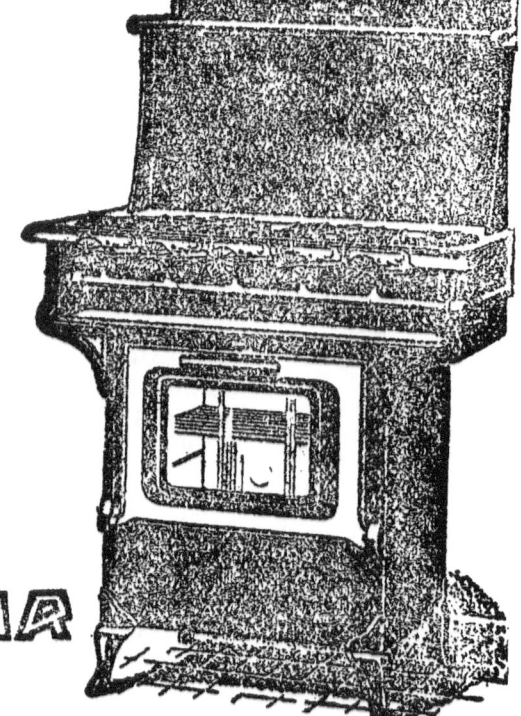

KOLMEIER & KLIER CO.

Peter's Confectionery and Cafe

Fredericksburg, Texas.

Walter Peter, Manager.

OPERA HOUSE AND DANCE HALL.

Moving Picture Show in Connection.

A pleasant place where you and your friends are always welcome.

Your Patronage appreciated!

ROBERT S. KLETT

Phone No. 4. Fredericksburg, Texas.

For perfect results and satisfaction on Baking Day, use:

"Bob White", "Liberty Bell" & "Hearts Delight" Flour

Model Tailor Shop

Cleaning, Pressing, Dyeing, Altering,
and Repairing for Ladies and Gentlemen. All work called for and delivered.
Satisfaction Guaranteed. Phone 70.

CONTENTS.

Relishes .... 9 to 12
Soups .... 13 to 17
Oysters and Fish .... 18 to 22
Poultry and Game .... 23 to 28
Meats .... 29 to 38
Macaroni and Rice .... 39 to 42
Pancakes 43
Eggs, Potatoes, etc .... 39 to 45
Vegetables .... 46 to 55
Salads and Salad Dressings .... 56 to 69
Puddings .... 70 to 77
Pastry, Pies and Tarts .... 78 to 88
Bread .... 89 to 92
Yeast Cakes .... 90 to 91
Coffee Cake, Rolls, Doughnuts and Gems ...... 92 to 96
Cookies .... 97 to 111
Layer Cakes and Frostings .... 112 to 126
Loaf Cakes .... 127 to 141
Extra Hints 142
Sandwiches .... 143 to 145
Confectionery .... 146 to 151
Jellies and Preserves .... 152 to 154
Catsups, Pickles, etc. .... 155 to 165